THE SIMON & SCHUSTER

BOOK
PLANET
EARTH

SIMON & SCHUSTER BOOKS FOR YOUNG READERS
Simon & Schuster Building, Rockefeller Center
1230 Avenue of the Americas, New York, New York 10020
. Copyright © 1991 by Grisewood & Dempsey Ltd.
All rights reserved including the right of reproduction
in whole or in part in any form.
Originally published in Great Britain by Kingfisher Books.
First U.S. edition 1992
SIMON & SCHUSTER BOOKS FOR YOUNG READERS
is a trademark of Simon & Schuster.
Manufactured in Spain

10 9 8 7 6 5 4 3 2 1   (pbk) 10 9 8 7 6 5 4 3 2 1

Library of Congress Cataloging-in-Publication Data
Bramwell, Martyn. The Simon & Schuster young readers' book of planet earth /
by Martyn Bramwell. p. cm. Summary: Discusses Earth's place in
the solar system, its atmosphere, weather, geology, oceans,
natural history, and environmental issues. 1. Earth—Juvenile
literature. [1. Earth.] I. Title. II. Title: Simon and Schuster young
readers' book of planet earth. QB631.4.B73 1992 550—dc20 91-38216 CIP
ISBN 0-671-77830-7   ISBN 0-671-77831-5 (pbk)

Edited by Veronica Pennycook
Picture research by Elaine Willis and Su Alexander
Index by Isabelle Paton
Designed by David Jefferis and Nigel Osborne
Phototypeset by Southern Positives and Negatives
   (SPAN), Lingfield, Surrey
Printed in Spain

BOOK OF PLANET EARTH

BY MARTYN BRAMWELL

SIMON & SCHUSTER BOOKS FOR YOUNG READERS
Published by Simon & Schuster
New York · London · Toronto · Sydney · Tokyo · Singapore

Contents

THE BLUE PLANET 6
Earth's Family 8
Earth's Satellite: the Moon 12
Eclipses 16
Measuring Time 18

THE RESTLESS ATMOSPHERE 24
Atmospheric Layers 26
The Weather Machine 29
Highs and Lows 34
Weather Systems 36
Cloud, Mist, and Dew 40
Rain, Hail, and Snow 44
Lightning and Thunder 47
Storms 50
Meteorologists at Work 54

THE EARTH UNDER OUR FEET 56
The Structure of the Earth 58
Rocks and Landscapes 61
The Rock Cycle 70
Earth's Changing Face 72
Rocks Under Pressure 78
Earthquakes 80
Geophysical Prospecting 83
Fossils 86

THE OCEANS 90
The Ocean Basins 92
Exploring the Oceans 95
World Oceans and Seas 98
Ocean Currents 100
Waves 104
Tides 107
The Ocean Resource 110

THE LIVING EARTH 114
Patterns of Climate 116
Vegetation and Soil 120
The Water Cycle 124
World Rivers and Lakes 126
Nature's Recycling System 128
Energy from the Sun 130
Food Chains and Webs 132
Parasites and Partnerships 136

ISSUES OF TODAY 140
The People Problem 142
Raw Materials and Energy 148
Alternative Energy 152
The Loss of the Forests 154
Soil Erosion 160
Air Pollution 164
The Greenhouse Effect 168
The Waste Problem 170
The Threat to Wildlife 174
Conservation in Action 178

Glossary 180
Index 186

The Blue Planet

Viewed from far out in Space, the Earth is one of the most beautiful of all the known planets. The oceans, which cover 70 percent of its surface, and the clouds, which constantly swirl over land and sea, reflect the Sun's light so that the planet shines bright and blue against the blackness of Space. But it was not always like this.

The story of our home planet, and the other eight planets that make up our Solar System, began more than 6 billion years ago in a vast cloud of interstellar gas and dust drifting through Space. Slowly, the cloud began to collapse inward as the tiny particles of dust were pulled toward each other by the force of gravity. The center of the cloud became more and more dense, and as it did so the temperature and pressure inside it rose higher and higher. Eventually nuclear reactions set in, and a new star – the Sun – began to blaze in Space.

Around the new star other parts of the cloud collapsed into smaller masses of dust, gas, and ice. Closest to the Sun, the fierce heat drove off most of the gases, and the dust clouds were crushed and compressed into four small, dense, solid planets. Farther away, where the heat was less intense, the clouds formed the much bigger outer planets, which even today consist mainly of the gases hydrogen and helium.

As the primitive Earth was crushed by gravity, heat and pressure melted the dust. The heavier metals, iron and nickel, sank to the center, forming a molten core, while lighter minerals formed a thin skin of rock floating on the surface. The Earth was born 4.6 billion years ago, but almost 1.6 billion years were to pass before the first sign of life appeared on its surface.

▶ **The NASA space flights** have provided many spectacular photographs of our planet, and among the most beautiful are those showing the swirling masses of cloud that trace the pattern of weather systems across the face of the globe.

Earth's Family

The four innermost planets in the Solar System are solid, but only Earth has water on its surface and a life-supporting atmosphere. Mercury and Venus are closer to the Sun and too hot for life. Mars is farther away and too cold.

Beyond these inner planets lies the asteroid belt, a zone of rocks and miniplanets ranging in size from a few feet to several hundred miles across. Farther out are the four gas giants – Jupiter, Saturn, Uranus, and Neptune – which are huge frozen worlds of hydrogen, helium, and other gases. And beyond them all lies Pluto, a tiny ball of dust and ice spinning through space like a dirty snowball, almost 4 billion miles from the Sun.

THE SOLAR SYSTEM

1: Mercury is about 3,025 mi in diameter. It has no moons, and no atmosphere.

2: Venus is 7,500 mi in diameter. It has no moons and a dense atmosphere of carbon dioxide gas.

3: Earth is 7,910 mi in diameter. It has one moon and an atmosphere made mainly of nitrogen and oxygen.

4: Mars is about 4,220 mi across. It has 2 moons and a thin atmosphere made of carbon dioxide.

5: Jupiter is 88,500 mi across. It has 17 or more moons and one faint ring.

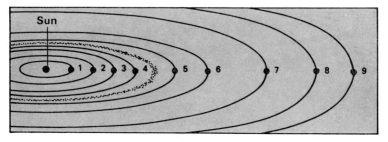

▲ All the planets travel around the Sun in the same direction, on paths, or orbits, that are oval in shape. From the Sun outward, the order is Mercury, Venus, Earth, Mars, asteroids, Jupiter, Saturn, Uranus, Neptune, and Pluto.

9: Pluto is about 1,365 mi across. It has one small moon. Very little is known about this planet.

7: Uranus is 32,240 mi in diameter. It has vertical rings and 15 faint moons.

6: Saturn is 74,400 mi in diameter. It has 24 moons and several bright rings.

8: Neptune is 30,250 mi in diameter. It has 6 moons and several rings.

The Sun is by far the largest body in the Solar System.

Sun

Moon

▲ **The Sun's diameter is** 863,000 mi, which is 109 times that of the Earth. At 7,910 mi, the Earth's diameter is 3.67 times that of its satellite, the Moon.

Earth

The Sun

The Sun's surface is very hot – about 11,000°F. The source of this heat lies deep inside the Sun where nuclear reactions change hydrogen gas into helium gas. These nuclear reactions release vast amounts of energy, which keep the temperature at the center of the Sun at about 25,000,000°F. This energy travels to the Sun's surface where it keeps the outer layers in a constant state of motion.

Dark spots on the surface are whirlpools of gas that appear dark because they are about 3,600°F cooler than the surrounding surface. Although the surface of the Sun appears very bright to us, and it is too dangerous to look at directly, the Sun's center is even hotter.

Because of its distance from the Sun, the Earth is the only planet that is neither too hot nor too cold for life. Plants and animals depend entirely on the Sun's heat for energy, and so life on Earth should last for as long

as the Sun shines. But that will not be forever. Like all stars, the Sun will eventually use up all its hydrogen and have no more energy left to give out. The core of helium will have expanded so much that it will collapse in on itself, and the Sun will explode, engulfing the Solar System in a huge fireball. Fortunately for us, that will not happen for at least another 5 billion years.

The Milky Way

The Sun may seem very special to us, but in Space terms it is nothing more than a very ordinary, medium-sized star among the 100 billion stars that make up our local galaxy – the Milky Way. And beyond this, there are millions of other galaxies in the Universe, some of them even larger than the Milky Way.

Look up into the sky on a clear, dark night, and the Milky Way appears as a concentrated band of stars spanning the heavens. We see it like this since we are looking along the flattened edge of the galaxy where millions of stars all lie in the same direction. If we could see it from far out in Space, the Milky Way would look more like a spiral with a thick central hub.

Our Sun and its cluster of planets lie about two-thirds of the way out from the center, on one of the long spiral arms. (In the diagram below the position of the Sun is shown by a black circle.) The whole galaxy is rotating around the central hub, and it takes the Solar System approximately 225 million years to make one complete revolution.

Distances in Space are so great that they are measured in light-years. A light-year is the distance traveled by a ray of light in one year, roughly 6 trillion miles. The Milky Way is about 100,000 light-years across – and it is not even a particularly big galaxy!

◀ **The Milky Way** would appear something like this if seen from out in Space.

▼ **From the Earth** we look sideways at an arm of the spiral.

Earth's Satellite: the Moon

Satellites are small heavenly bodies that orbit larger bodies, such as the planets. The Earth has one satellite, the Moon, and because it is only 238,000 mi away, and clearly visible from Earth with the naked eye, it is the most familiar of all the heavenly bodies.

The Moon creates no light of its own. It shines by reflecting the light of the Sun. Looking up from the Earth, we see only the part of the Moon that is currently being lit by the Sun, and as the Moon is traveling around the Earth on its near-circular orbit, the brightly lit part of the Moon's surface constantly changes shape, from the fully lit disc of the Full Moon to the darkened face of the New Moon. We call this changing pattern the phases of the Moon. The Moon orbits the Earth in just over 29 days, so this is how long it takes for each cycle of the Moon's phases.

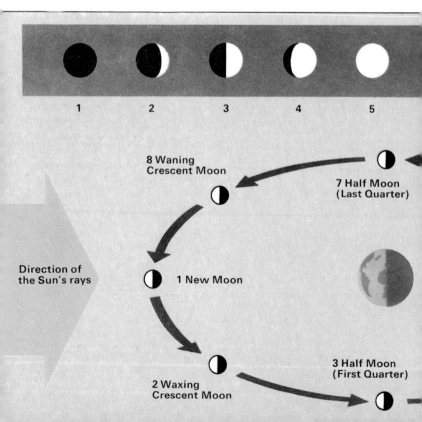

The Moon's phases

A New Moon occurs when the Moon is directly in between the Sun and the Earth. At this time the far side of the Moon is lit by the Sun but the side facing the Earth is in total darkness, and the Moon can barely be seen. After a few days the Moon's orbit carries it out of the direct line to the Sun and we can see a thin crescent lit by the Sun's rays.

As the Moon continues around the Earth, more and more of its face is illuminated. A week after the New Moon, half the face is lit, and a week later the Moon has traveled halfway around the Earth so that it is facing the Sun and fully lit. This is the stage we call the Full Moon. From that point onward the illuminated section gets smaller and smaller as the Moon wanes toward the next New Moon.

The Moon's influence

The ever-changing phases of the Moon have some surprising effects on the world around us. The tides, for example, are produced by a combination of the Sun and Moon's gravity pulling at the water in the ocean basins. According to the position of the Moon in its orbit, we get either the very high spring tides, or the much lower neap tides (see page 108).

Animals also react to the Moon's cycle. Some fish, such as grunion, spawn only at the Full and New Moons, wriggling ashore in their millions on the beaches of the Pacific coast. There they lay their eggs in the wet sand at the high-tide mark. The eggs hatch just in time for the young fish to be washed into

6   7   8

6 Waning
Gibbous Moon

5 Full Moon

4 Waxing
Gibbous Moon

◀ **When the Moon is between** the Earth and the Sun (1), its far side is lit and the near side is in darkness. We call this the New Moon. When the Moon is at the far side of its orbit (5), we see its face fully illuminated, and this is the Full Moon. At stages in between we see only the segment of the Moon's surface that is reflecting the Sun's light.

13

the sea by the next high tides two weeks later.

In many mammals the female's reproductive cycle is linked to the phases of the Moon. Wildebeest on the African savannas mate during the Full Moon, and this ensures that all the calves are born within a few days of each other during the herd's annual migration. The great advantage of this is that with thousands of calves around at the same time there is a limit to the number that can be killed by predators.

Reaching for the Moon

As it orbits the Earth, the Moon turns slowly on its own axis – an imaginary line drawn through its center – making one complete revolution in just over 29 days. This is the same as the time taken by the Moon to make one complete journey around the Earth.

▲ **Harrison Schmitt,** collecting samples of rock and dust with the "lunar rake" during the *Apollo 17* Moon mission.

The result is that the same side of the Moon is always turned toward the Earth. Centuries-old maps of the Moon show us the same features on the face of the Moon that we can see today. It was not until the USSR's space-craft *Luna 3* photographed the back of the Moon in October 1959 that the hidden side was seen for the first time.

These initial photographic missions to the Moon were followed by a series of soft landings by automatic probes. *Luna 16*, launched by the USSR in 1970, was the first probe to land on the Moon, take samples, and then return safely to Earth. But it was the U.S.'s Apollo program that

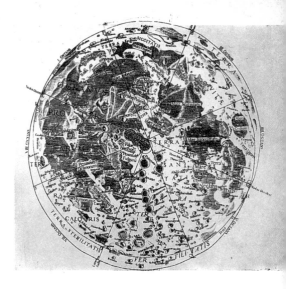

► **Riccioli's Moon**
map of 1651 shows the
main maria (now
known to be lava fields,
not seas) as dark areas,
and it names many of
the major craters. The
naming system that
Riccioli devised is still
in use today.

first managed to land people on the Moon.

On December 21, 1968, *Apollo 8* blasted off carrying three U.S. astronauts who circled the Moon ten times, at one stage only 68 mi above the surface. This and *Apollo 10* were the final tests. On July 21, 1969, the first manned landing on the Moon was made when Neil Armstrong and Edwin Aldrin stepped out onto the Sea of Tranquillity, while Michael Collins orbited above them in *Apollo 11*'s command module, *Columbia*.

MOON FACTS

Diameter:	2,160 mi
Average distance from Earth:	238,857 mi
Maximum distance from Earth:	252,710 mi
Minimum distance from Earth:	221,463 mi
Mass:	0.012 × Earth's mass
Density:	3.3 × density of water
Lunar month:	29.53 days
Surface gravity:	0.167 × Earth's gravity
Atmosphere:	None
Daily temperature range (Equator):	3,600°F

Eclipses

There are two kinds of eclipse: an eclipse of the Sun, or solar eclipse, which happens when the Moon passes in front of the Sun and blocks its light to the Earth, and an eclipse of the Moon, or lunar eclipse, which is when the Moon passes into the Earth's shadow.

In many ancient civilizations a solar eclipse was thought to be an omen of terrible misfortunes. The Moon can block out our view of the Sun completely, plunging the Earth into darkness and leaving visible only the shimmering halo of the Sun's hot gas atmosphere. The total solar eclipse of June 1955 lasted for 7 minutes and 8 seconds – the longest in 1,238 years. Total lunar eclipses, on the other hand, may last for up to 1 hour and 40 minutes.

Sun   Moon   Earth

Umbra   Penumbra

▲ **A solar eclipse** occurs when the Moon passes across the face of the Sun and casts its shadow onto the Earth's surface. A total eclipse will be seen by observers in the central area of dense shadow, the umbra, while a partial eclipse is seen by those in the larger outer shadow zone, or penumbra.

◄ **In a total eclipse,** the Sun's disk cannot be seen, but the faint outer atmosphere shines out around the lunar outline.

▼ A lunar eclipse occurs when the Moon passes into the long and relatively wide shadow cast by the Earth. It is the Moon's small size compared with the width of the shadow that makes lunar eclipses last so long.

▲ The four stages in a lunar eclipse, with the Earth's shadow passing across the face of the Moon from lower left to upper right. This journey can take up to 6 hours, with total eclipse lasting for as long as 1 hour 40 minutes.

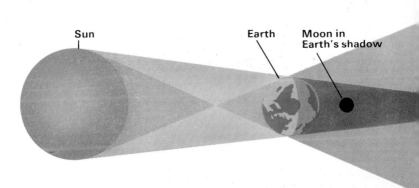

Sun   Earth   Moon in Earth's shadow

Measuring Time

We measure time by means of the two main motions of the Earth. One is the rotation of the Earth on its own axis – an imaginary line running through the center of the planet from pole to pole; the other is the Earth's orbital journey around the Sun. The first of these motions defines the length of the day, and the second defines the year and also the seasons (see pages 22–23).

Adjusting Time

The Earth completes one circuit around the Sun in 365 days, 5 hours, 48 minutes, and 46 seconds – a period known as the solar year. However, this is not a very convenient unit for everyday use, so the calendar year is divided into 365 days, with an extra day in every fourth year (the leap year) to catch up the missing quarter-days and prevent us from getting out of step with the Sun.

The length of a day also needs some adjustment for everyday use. According to the Sun, an average day is 24 hours, 3 minutes, and 56 seconds long, measured from the time the Sun is overhead at a point on the Equator until the next time it reaches precisely the same point. Unfortunately, as the Earth rotates on its axis it wobbles a bit, and this makes the length of the natural day not quite regular – so we now use a standard day of 24 hours, made up of 86,400 seconds.

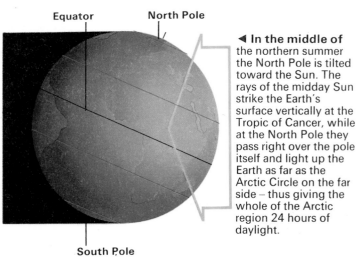

Equator   North Pole

South Pole

◀ **In the middle of** the northern summer the North Pole is tilted toward the Sun. The rays of the midday Sun strike the Earth's surface vertically at the Tropic of Cancer, while at the North Pole they pass right over the pole itself and light up the Earth as far as the Arctic Circle on the far side – thus giving the whole of the Arctic region 24 hours of daylight.

Day and night

The Earth's axis is not upright – it is tilted over at $23\frac{1}{2}°$ to the vertical. This has a huge effect on the length of day and night at different points on the Earth's surface, because it means that the Sun's rays strike the Earth unevenly. It is only at the Equator that the day is divided evenly into 12 hours of daylight and 12 hours of darkness.

▲ The midnight Sun is seen in polar regions during the six months of daylight.

During winter in the Northern Hemisphere, the North Pole is tilted away from the Sun, and everywhere within the Arctic Circle has six months of darkness. At the same time, the South Pole is tilted toward the Sun, giving it six months of daylight.

▶ During the northern winter the North Pole is tilted away from the Sun, giving the Arctic region 24 hours of darkness. It is the Tropic of Capricorn's turn to have the Sun overhead at midday and the Antarctic region to have 24 hours of daylight. Between the extremes of the North and South Poles, the length of the day varies with the distance from the Equator.

Tropic of Cancer   Arctic Circle

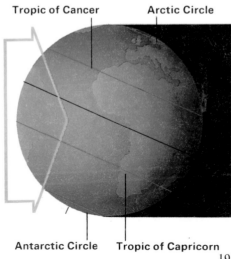

Antarctic Circle   Tropic of Capricorn

19

Time zones

Mapmakers divide the Earth's surface into a series of thin segments, rather like the pieces of an orange. Each segment is 1° wide, measured from the Earth's center. So looking down on the North Pole there are 360 of these lines of longitude fanning out from the pole and sweeping over the Earth's surface to meet again at the South Pole.

The Earth rotates from west to east, so we see the Sun rising in the east and setting in the west. Since the Earth takes 24 hours to make one complete revolution, traveling 1° east or west will make a difference of four minutes in local time. Traveling west means putting the clock back, while going east means putting it forward. However, resetting your watch every time you crossed a line of longitude would be very inconvenient, so to simplify matters the world is divided into 24 time zones.

Each of these time zones represents one hour. They are set at 15° intervals, which is the distance in longitude that the Sun appears to travel every hour, but the time zones zigzag around many country borders so that within a country all clocks will show the same time. However, in very large countries such as Canada, the U.S., and the USSR, there are several time zones. For example, when it is noon in Los Angeles, it is 2 p.m. in Dallas and 3 p.m. in New York.

All the lines of longitude are measured from the 0° line, which runs through Greenwich in London and is called the Greenwich Meridian. All the time zones, too, are measured from this starting point. When it is noon in Greenwich, it is morning west of Greenwich and afternoon to the east – the exact time of day depends on how far west or east.

At the opposite side of the Earth from Greenwich, at longitude 180°, lies the International Date Line. Here, the time is 12 hours different from Greenwich, and as a ship or plane crosses the line, the date changes by exactly one day.

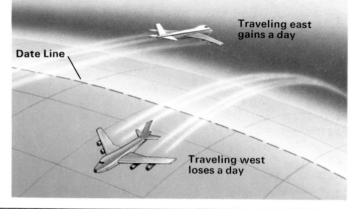

CROSSING THE INTERNATIONAL DATE LINE

The International Date Line is the only place on Earth where you can stand with one foot in Sunday and the other in Monday.

Air travelers flying over it from east to west lose a full day, whereas those traveling from west to east gain a full day.

Traveling east gains a day

Date Line

Traveling west loses a day

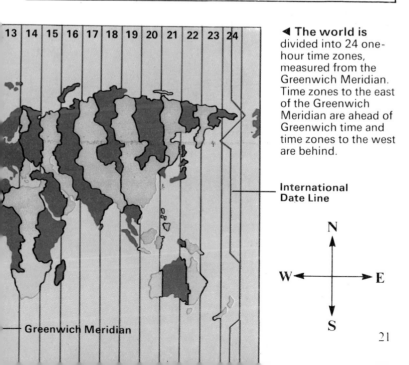

◄ **The world is** divided into 24 one-hour time zones, measured from the Greenwich Meridian. Time zones to the east of the Greenwich Meridian are ahead of Greenwich time and time zones to the west are behind.

International Date Line

Greenwich Meridian

The Changing Seasons

As the Earth orbits the Sun its axis always remains pointing toward the same spot in outer Space. As we have seen, this means that at one point on the orbit the North Pole is tilted toward the Sun, while at the opposite end of the orbit the North Pole is tilted away from the Sun. It is this changing orientation that produces the seasons.

On June 21 the North Pole reaches its maximum tilt toward the Sun. This is called the summer solstice and it marks the beginning of summer in the Northern Hemisphere and winter in the Southern Hemisphere. On December 21 the North Pole is tilted away from the Sun, thus creating the winter solstice which marks the onset of the Northern Hemisphere winter. The midway points are March 21 and September 23, and these are called the spring and autumn equinoxes. On these dates, day and night are equal in length at all places lying at the same latitude, or distance from the Equator.

At any particular time of the year, the amount of daylight and general climatic conditions in

▼ As the Earth hurtles around its orbit at up to 18 mi/sec, its ever-changing angle to the Sun produces the seasons.

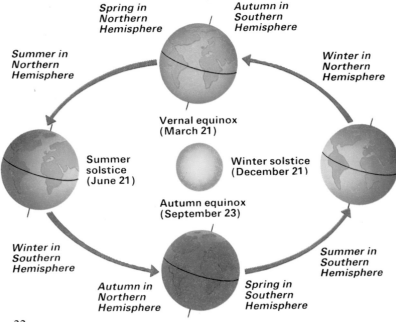

Spring in Northern Hemisphere

Autumn in Southern Hemisphere

Summer in Northern Hemisphere

Winter in Northern Hemisphere

Vernal equinox (March 21)

Summer solstice (June 21)

Winter solstice (December 21)

Autumn equinox (September 23)

Winter in Southern Hemisphere

Summer in Southern Hemisphere

Autumn in Northern Hemisphere

Spring in Southern Hemisphere

the Southern Hemisphere are roughly the opposite of those in the North. Autumn in Europe coincides with spring in South Africa, and so on through the annual cycle of the seasons.

Seasonal cycles

The globe can be roughly divided into three broad zones with very different seasonal cycles. The greatest seasonal variation of all is found in the polar zone, especially in the Arctic wilderness. Here, the long, cold winter alter-nates with a brief summer when mosses, lichens, and herbs cover the ground. Farther south lies the temperate zone. Typically this has four well-marked seasons, with a moderately cold winter and a warm summer separated by mild spring and autumn seasons. Finally there is the tropical zone, where the Sun remains high in the sky all year-round. Here, the constant rain and sunshine pro-duce abundant plant growth, and there is little difference be-tween the seasons.

▶ **In summer the** Arctic tundra is covered in a dense low carpet of mosses, lichens, grasses, and tough, heatherlike shrubs. There is plenty of food for birds, from flies and mosquitoes to a huge variety of seeds and berries, like these blueberries on the Alaskan tundra.

◀ **Tundra plants** must be exceptionally hardy to survive the long months of bitter cold. In winter the tundra soil is frozen solid to a depth of many feet.

23

The Restless Atmosphere

The Earth is surrounded by a layer of gas and water vapor which we call the atmosphere. For almost 2 billion years the Earth's atmosphere consisted mainly of carbon dioxide, methane, and ammonia – a poisonous mixture of gases which no living creature could possibly have breathed. But with the arrival of the first plant cells, a slow yet vital change began. Almost all plants live by using a process called photosynthesis – they use the energy in sunlight and the carbon dioxide in the air to make food. Oxygen is given off as a by-product. So when these first plant cells started the process of photosynthesis, oxygen began to be released into the Earth's atmosphere.

For many more millions of years this oxygen was used up as fast as it was produced, because it immediately combined with other gases in the air and with minerals in the rocks of the Earth's primitive crust. Eventually, however, these chemical processes slowed down and there was oxygen to spare. It could not escape into Space because, like the other gases in the atmosphere, it was held close to the Earth's surface by the pull of gravity. Gradually, the amount of oxygen built up as more and more plants evolved, until today roughly one-fifth of our modern atmosphere is oxygen and four-fifths is nitrogen.

Very early on, some of the oxygen drifted high into the upper levels of the atmosphere. There, it was bombarded by the Sun's radiation and converted into ozone, which formed a protective screen against the ultraviolet radiation of the Sun. Without the protection of this ozone layer, animal life could not have evolved, and if we damage it now, future generations will be faced with one of the most serious environmental problems imaginable.

▶ **Even the most dramatic** clouds consist of nothing more than water droplets or ice crystals, shaped by winds and temperature layers and lit by the Sun.

Atmospheric Layers

The Earth's atmosphere is surprisingly thin. It stretches about 400 miles up from the Earth's surface, but long before that height is reached it thins out so much that it is barely detectable. The force of gravity does far more than just prevent the atmosphere from floating off into Space – it actually squashes it down against the Earth.

Unlike liquids, gases can be compressed, or squeezed into a smaller space. The result is that about 80 percent of the gas in the atmosphere is contained within about 12 miles of the Earth's surface. In fact, the air thins out so quickly with increasing altitude, that even a few thousand feet above sea level we can feel the difference – and climbers on the world's highest mountains frequently have to carry additional oxygen supplies with them.

The chemical composition of the atmosphere also changes with height. Near the ground, oxygen and nitrogen make up 99 percent of its volume, with tiny amounts of other gases. Almost all the water vapor, and everything we know as weather, occurs in this region, within about 9 miles of the surface. At higher levels, the proportion of oxygen falls and helium appears in the mixture; and at the outer limits of the atmosphere, the mixture consists almost entirely of hydrogen and helium.

▲ **The atmosphere is a thin** coating around the Earth. It is no thicker than the skin of an apple when compared with the size of the planet.

▶ **The atmosphere** can be divided into four main layers. The exosphere is the outermost layer. It starts about 375 mi above the Earth and gradually thins out into Space. The ionosphere is the next layer. It begins about 50 mi up. The protective band of ozone, which absorbs dangerous ultraviolet light, lies in the next level, the stratosphere. The troposphere is the lowest level, in which all our weather occurs. It is about 5 mi thick at the poles and 9 mi thick near the Equator.

THE ATMOSPHERE

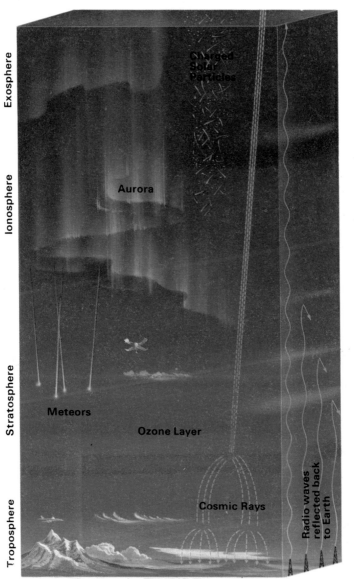

Exosphere

Ionosphere

Stratosphere

Troposphere

Charged Solar Particles

Aurora

Meteors

Ozone Layer

Cosmic Rays

Radio waves reflected back to Earth

Lights in the sky

Many beautiful phenomena can be explained when we understand the makeup of the atmosphere. Sunlight, water vapor, and solar particles all combine to create a great variety of optical effects in the sky.

One of the most famous is the "aurora," called the *aurora borealis* (northern lights) in the Northern Hemisphere and the *aurora australis* in the Southern Hemisphere. These dancing curtains and streaks of colored light are seen in polar skies. They are caused when streams of electrically charged solar particles, attracted to the magnetic field around the Earth's

▲ **The northern lights, or** *aurora borealis*, photographed in the far north of Alaska.

poles, collide with molecules of air in the ionosphere.

"Shooting stars" are the fiery trails of meteors burning up as they meet the resistance of the Earth's atmosphere. Most are quite small, but occasionally a large one has hit the Earth, leaving a huge scar like the 4,000-foot wide, 600-foot deep, Meteor Crater in Arizona.

In the lower atmosphere, sunlight shining through water droplets in the air may be split into its many colors, producing rainbows.

The Weather Machine

Everything we know as weather takes place in the lower atmosphere, where the gas is dense and where most of the water vapor is found. This ocean of gas and vapor is never still; it surges just like the deep oceans. Some of its movements cover large parts of the Earth's surface, others are quite small and localized. But large or small they have one thing in common – they are driven by the Sun.

Since the Earth is round, its surface is not evenly heated as it orbits the Sun. Near the Equator the Sun is almost overhead, while in higher latitudes its rays are spread over a much bigger area. The amount of heat absorbed by various areas of land and sea therefore varies, and so does the amount of heat transferred to the air above them. The result is that the atmosphere is not the same all over the globe; it consists of about 20 large air masses.

The temperature of each air mass, and the amount of moisture it contains, depends on the land or sea area over which it formed. For example, the air mass that forms over the Sahara Desert is typically hot and dry, while the one that drifts across the North Atlantic Ocean is generally warm and moist. The boundary zones between air masses are called frontal zones, and these are often the site of unstable weather.

▼ **The Sun's heat is strongest** in the Tropics where the Sun is almost overhead. In temperate regions the curvature of the globe spreads the Sun's rays over a larger area. Nearer the poles, the Sun's rays strike the surface at an angle, so the heat is weaker.

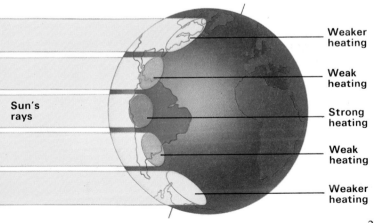

Sun's rays

Weaker heating

Weak heating

Strong heating

Weak heating

Weaker heating

29

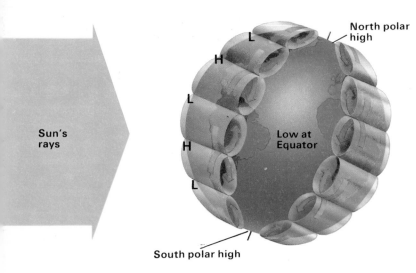

Sun's rays

North polar high

L H L H L

Low at Equator

South polar high

Atmospheric cells

Intense solar heating in the Tropics warms up the land and sea, and also the overlying air. Warm air is more buoyant than cool air, so the warm air close to the Earth's surface tends to rise. These rising columns of warm air spread out high in the atmosphere, where they cool down by radiating heat into Space. They then sink back toward the Earth,

▲ **In the six circulation cells,** air flows from high pressure areas to low pressure areas.

about 30° north and south of the Equator.

Warm air rising at the Equator creates an area of low air pressure. The descending currents of cool air lying to the north and south of the Equator create bands of high air pressure.

▶ **This diagram** shows the main wind systems: the trade winds, the westerlies, and the polar easterlies. Compare it with the diagram above to see that winds blow toward areas of low pressure.

Between these main winds lie regions of light winds.

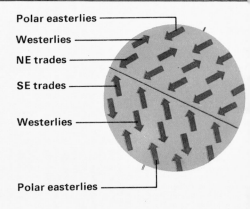

Polar easterlies

Westerlies

NE trades

SE trades

Westerlies

Polar easterlies

At ground level, cool air moves from the high pressure zones to the low pressure zone. This movement forms two circulation cells, or circles of matching air flows, one on each side of the Equator. Outside these two cells lie four more circulation cells in the temperate and polar regions. In each cell, descending air creates high pressure zones, and rising warmer air creates low pressure zones.

Winds

Winds are the movement of air from areas of high pressure to areas of low pressure. The circulation cells create the Earth's three main wind systems. The trade winds are formed by the cells on either side of the Equator. The westerlies are winds produced in the temperate regions, and the polar easterlies are formed in the far north and south.

▲ The dominant wind direction is frequently revealed by the distorted growth of trees in exposed places.

The Coriolis force

It is clear from the diagram of the main wind systems on page 30 that winds do not blow straight from areas of high pressure to areas of low pressure along lines of longitude. All the main winds blow at an angle across the face of the globe, and this is due to the Coriolis force. Any object moving freely over the surface of the Earth – whether it is a water molecule, air molecule, dust particle, or football – will be deflected to the right of its true course in the Northern Hemisphere and to the left in the Southern Hemisphere. This strange effect is caused by the fact that, as the particle moves over the Earth's surface, the globe itself is turning beneath it.

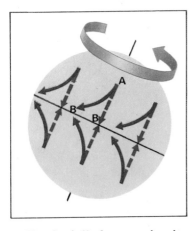

▲ **The Coriolis force makes it** look as if a moving object takes a curved course even when it is traveling direct from A to B. It is one of several factors that control the global pattern of winds.

Global wind patterns

Detailed weather records have been kept for many years, and this makes it possible to draw maps of average global wind and pressure patterns during the year.

The map below shows the pressure and wind pattern in July. The distribution of land and sea, and also the presence of mountain ranges and other features, all combine to make the real pattern less regular than the theoretical pattern shown on page 30. But the main areas of high and low pressure are clear to see, with the trade winds and westerlies sweeping in curved tracks from high pressure areas to low, under the effect of the Coriolis force.

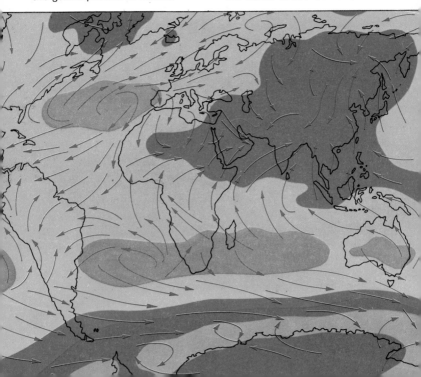

The main surface currents of the oceans are driven by the wind, and the link between the two can immediately be seen by comparing this map with the map of the currents on pages 100–101. The clockwise swirl of winds around the Northern Hemisphere high pressure areas, and the counterclockwise direction of winds around the Southern Hemisphere high pressure areas, are almost perfectly matched by the great ocean current systems.

Special winds

In many parts of the world a combination of the weather pattern and the shape of the land produces a particular kind of wind which always blows at a particular time of the year. These are known as local winds.

One of the best-known local winds is the chinook of North America. This wind blows from the west in spring. As it blows in from the Pacific Ocean, the air rises over the Rockies and most of its moisture falls as rain. The wind then pours down the east side of the Rockies on to the plains. By now it is dry, and so warm that it melts the snow – and that is how it got its name: Chinook is an Indian word meaning "snow-eater." There is a similar kind of wind in South Africa which is known as the berg. It, too, rises to pass over a high plateau and then brings the heat down to the lower levels.

An important family of winds occurs in the Mediterranean region. These winds form when low pressure systems travel west to east through the Mediterranean Sea. The low pressure draws in warm, dry air from the Sahara, producing the sirocco wind in North Africa and Italy, and the hot khamsin in Egypt.

◄ **Average world air** pressures and wind patterns for July.

AIR PRESSURE IN MILLIBARS

— 990
— 1000
— 1010
— 1020

33

Highs and Lows

The two main air pressure systems that control our weather are highs and lows. Highs are produced when relatively cool, heavy air sinks down toward the Earth's surface. The weight of the descending air increases the pressure at the surface and this produces a high barometer reading. When it reaches the ground the air spreads out in a spiral, rotating clockwise in the Northern Hemisphere and counterclockwise in the Southern Hemisphere.

Lows occur where warm air rises, decreasing the pressure at the surface and giving a low barometer reading. This air is replaced by air flowing in from neighboring areas of higher pressure. Again the system forms a spiral, but this spiral flows inward. And in the Northern Hemisphere the wind direction is counterclockwise around the low pressure area, while south of the Equator it is clockwise.

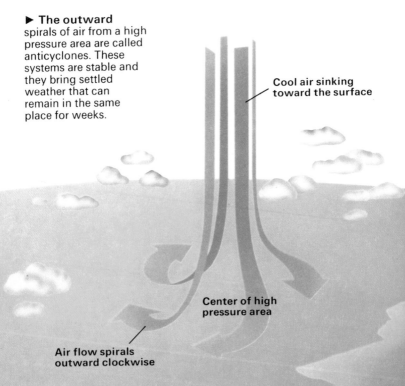

► **The outward** spirals of air from a high pressure area are called anticyclones. These systems are stable and they bring settled weather that can remain in the same place for weeks.

Cool air sinking toward the surface

Center of high pressure area

Air flow spirals outward clockwise

Contrasting weather

The main characteristic of the downward-moving air in a high pressure system is that it is cooler than the surrounding air. This makes it stable and unlikely to cause sudden changes in the weather. Clouds formed at higher levels generally dissolve as the air descends, leaving the sky clear and bright. These systems usually bring fine, settled weather, and are often more than 900 miles across. In summer they can bring long spells of hot dry weather; in winter they often produce the opposite extreme, with low temperatures, icy winds, clear nights, and hard frosts.

In a low pressure system, warm air rises like a bubble through surrounding air that is much cooler. This is a very unstable situation because the warm air will continue to rise for as long as it is warmer than its surroundings. It may not cool down to match the surrounding air until it has climbed to 30,000 feet or more. A rising mass of warm, damp air often produces towering storm clouds, with heavy rain and gusty winds, and possibly thunder, lightning, and hail.

▶ **Air spiraling** inward to a low pressure area is known as a cyclone, or depression. These unstable systems often bring periods of unsettled weather with rain and wind.

Warm air rising

Center of low pressure area

Air flow spirals inward counterclockwise

Weather Systems

Most of the weather that affects Western Europe is carried in from the west on weather systems that start life far out in the North Atlantic Ocean. Similar systems are carried into the western parts of North America, having started life in the North Pacific Ocean.

The birthplace of these weather systems is the boundary zone between the warm air masses lying over the oceans and the very cold air mass that lies to the north, over the Arctic region. This boundary zone is called the polar front. As the warm and cold air masses move past each other, small waves or kinks form along the boundary. And if conditions are right, the kink may develop into a full-scale depression.

The polar front

Depressions that form on the polar front usually develop in families of four or five. Each one drags the front farther south. But the families are often separated by high pressure systems that break the sequence, returning the front to its normal position.

▶ **The polar front lies in a** broad zone stretching right across the North Atlantic.

A DEVELOPING FRONT

Along the boundary zone between warm and cold air masses a kink may form as the warm air rises and the colder air pushes underneath it. This kink can develop into a triangular wedge of warm, moist air trapped between the two air masses. The winds start to rotate, and warm and cold fronts develop. A warm front marks the beginning edge of the warm air mass and a cold front marks the leading edge of the cold air mass.

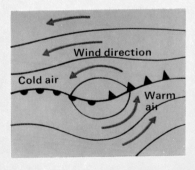

▲ **The system starts as a kink** on the polar front as warm air overrides colder polar air.

The life of a depression

Once the initial low pressure center has developed, and the winds have started to rotate around it, the depression is fully formed and it will drift eastward until it meets land, often bringing unsettled weather.

First to arrive is the warm front, usually announced by incoming layers of very high cloud (see next page). This front is followed by the warm sector – a pocket of warmer air trapped by the curved V-shape of the two fronts. And this in turn is followed by the cold front, which marks the rear edge of the depression.

Eventually, the cold front catches up with the warm front and either rides up over it or pushes its way underneath it. Either way, the warm sector is squeezed out and lifted clear of the ground. At this stage the front is described as an occluded front.

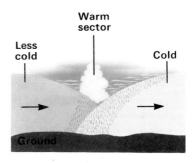

▲ **A warm occlusion occurs** when the advancing cold front rides up over the warm front.

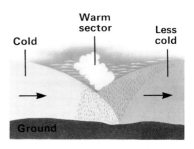

▲ **A cold occlusion occurs** when the advancing cold front undercuts the warm front.

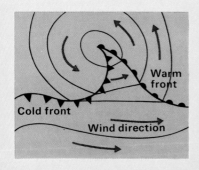

▲ **The system starts to rotate.** Warm and cold fronts develop and the depression deepens.

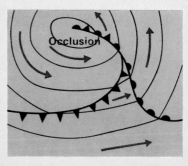

▲ **Eventually the cold front** catches up with the warm front and an occlusion occurs.

Frontal weather

The first sign that a warm front is approaching is usually given by high cirrus clouds, often at an altitude of 33,000 feet or more. The warm front slopes at quite a shallow angle, so these clouds may be 600 miles or more ahead of the front itself.

As the system moves nearer, layer upon layer of cloud appears, each layer lower than the last. The wispy cirrus clouds are followed by continuous sheets of cirrostratus, then altostratus (a medium-height layer-cloud), and finally, nimbostratus (the very low, dark cloud from which heavy rain is likely to fall). Some rain or snow may start to fall much earlier, from the altostratus, but this usually evaporates before it reaches the ground. The rain from the nimbostratus does no such thing. It usually pours down continuously, starting up to 200 miles ahead of the front and not easing until the front itself has passed through.

As the warm sector arrives

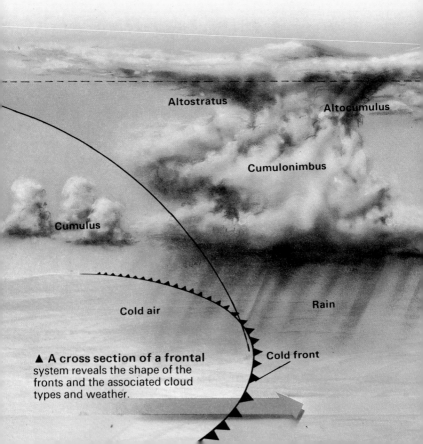

▲ A cross section of a frontal system reveals the shape of the fronts and the associated cloud types and weather.

overhead the skies partially clear, the wind shifts round, and the air feels much warmer. But the improvement does not last. The much steeper cold front then arrives, with towering cumulus and cumulonimbus clouds producing short, heavy showers accompanied by sudden gusts and changes in wind direction. If the cumulonimbus clouds are sufficiently large then thunderstorms may develop, with torrential rain or even violent showers of hailstones.

▲ **Satellite photographs of** depressions show clearly the curved lines of frontal cloud and the clear warm sector.

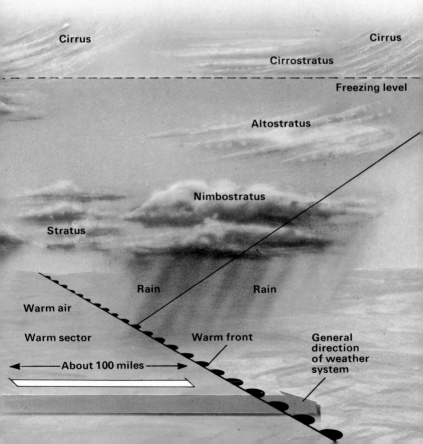

Cirrus

Cirrus

Cirrostratus

Freezing level

Altostratus

Nimbostratus

Stratus

Rain

Rain

Warm air

Warm sector

Warm front

General direction of weather system

◄— About 100 miles —►

Cloud, Mist, and Dew

Water vapor is present in the air around us all the time, mainly as an invisible gas. It only becomes visible when it condenses into liquid, not necessarily in large drops such as raindrops, but often as the microscopic droplets that float in the air to form mist, fog, clouds, or the haze that forms from your breath on a cold winter's day.

Just how much water there is in the air varies according to the place and to the temperature of the air. Warm air can carry more water vapor than cold air. If a mass of air is cooled, it will reach a point at which it can no longer hold all the water vapor it contains, and some of the moisture will condense out as droplets. Temperature falls with increasing altitude, and the level at which the water vapor is forced to condense into liquid droplets is marked by the base of the lowest cloud. Below that level, the air can cope with its load of water vapor, but higher up, in the cooler air, some of the vapor has to condense, thus forming clouds.

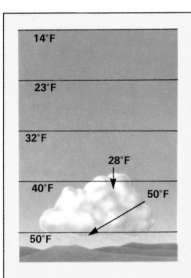 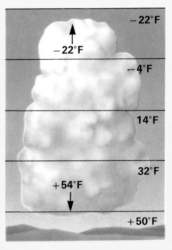

▲ **Stable cloud does not** rise upward and get bigger, because the air inside it is cooler than the surrounding air.

▲ **Unstable cloud is** warmer than the surrounding air and so it floats upward like a bubble, producing towering clouds.

How cloud and mist form

Two things are necessary for clouds, mist, fog, or dew to form. First, the air must contain enough water vapor; and second, something must cause the water vapor to condense. The two main causes of condensation are cooling of the air when it touches a cold surface, and cooling of the air when it is forced to rise.

After sunset, the land cools down quite quickly and the air in contact with the ground is also cooled. This can cause water to condense onto leaves, stones, and parked cars in the form of dew. If the temperature is below freezing, and the air is still, the water may be deposited as hoarfrost (frozen dew that forms a white coating on a surface). On warmer nights, when there is enough air

▲ **Table Mountain outside** Cape Town, in South Africa, is often covered by a layer of cloud that hangs over the edges just like a tablecloth.

movement to stir the air gently, the water may condense into fog or mist – cloud at ground level.

However, most clouds form where damp air is forced to rise above the condensation level. This often happens along the coast, when air moving in from the sea rises over the land. Mountains, too, often have caps of cloud, formed where the air flow is forced up and over the mountain barrier. In some cases, air forms waves after passing over a mountain. These waves may pass in and out of the condensation level repeatedly, creating a string of small clouds.

Types of cloud

Clouds are divided into three groups according to their height above the ground. In temperate regions, the high cirrus clouds usually form at between 16,000 and 42,000 feet; the medium clouds at between 6,500 and 23,000 feet; and the low clouds between ground level and about 6,500 feet. In polar regions, where the troposphere is only about 5 miles thick, the height ranges are a little lower; whereas in the Tropics, where the troposphere reaches up to about 9 miles, the height ranges are higher.

Cirrus clouds consist of ice crystals and they occur at high levels where the temperature is well below freezing. They are

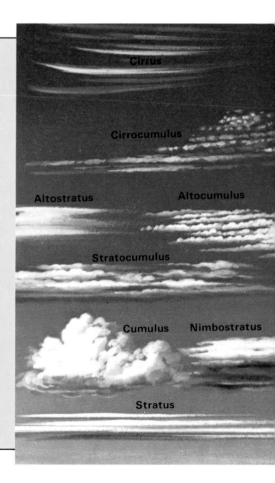

CLOUD TYPES

Cirrus: silky, white, hooked wisps of ice-crystal cloud.

Cirrostratus: thin, high sheets of cloud.

Cirrocumulus: thin, white layers of ice-cloud with ripples and rolls, often broken into small patches.

Altostratus: gray or bluish layer cloud, which often covers a large area of the sky.

Altocumulus: thicker white or gray layer cloud. It usually has ripples and waves.

silky in appearance and often form a thin veil across the sky. The medium- and low-level clouds consist of water droplets, and occur in two main types. One type is layered clouds, which may be thin enough for the Sun to shine through, such as altostratus; or thick, white, and fleecy, like altocumulus; or very thick, dark, and close to the ground, like the rain cloud nimbostratus. The other type consists of the dense, white "cauliflower" clouds, which usually have a small base but grow quite tall, and often have patches of clear sky between them. They range from the small, fluffy, fair-weather cumulus clouds of summer, to the huge cumulonimbus clouds that accompany cold fronts.

Cirrostratus

Cumulonimbus

Stratocumulus: lower-level layered cumulus cloud.

Cumulus: dense, white clouds, often with clear air between them.

Nimbostratus: thick, dark, layered cloud that usually brings rain or snow.

Stratus: layered cloud that is usually thin enough for the Sun to show through.

Cumulonimbus: very tall cloud that is white on top (often with a cap of cirrus), but low and dark at the base. It may bring heavy showers.

43

Rain, Hail, and Snow

Any water falling from a cloud, be it rain, sleet, hail, or snow, is known under the general term, precipitation. For the purposes of keeping weather records, all forms of precipitation are measured in inches of water.

Over the whole world, average annual precipitation is about 34 inches. However, the driest parts of the Sahara and Kalahari Deserts receive less than 1 inch, while at Calama in the Atacama Desert in Chile, rain has never even been recorded. At the other extreme, large areas within the Tropics have annual rainfall of over 80 inches, while parts of Colombia, India, Cameroon, and New Guinea receive well over 200 inches.

Why does it rain?
The water droplets that make up a cloud each measure only about 0.0008 inch in diameter and it may take up to a million of them to make one large raindrop. The cloud droplets are so light that they float in the air. They only begin to fall when they join together and become heavy enough for the force of gravity to pull them down against the resistance of the surrounding air.

Rain formation is really quite complex, and scientists now believe that there are two main processes. In temperate areas much of the rain starts in clouds that reach up to levels where the temperature is approximately −4°F to −40°F. At these levels, the cloud contains a mixture of water droplets and microscopic ice crystals. There is a constant process of change, with some of the ice melting, while at the same time more of the water droplets are freezing. The ice crystals grow bigger as they join together to form snowflakes. Eventually, the snowflakes become heavy enough to fall through the cloud. As they pass

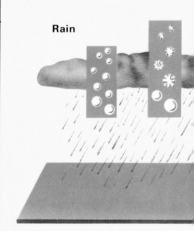

TYPES OF PRECIPITATION

Rain

▲ **Rain may form from** water droplets merging, or from melting snowflakes.

through the 32°F level they melt and continue falling as rain.

In tropical regions the clouds are often much warmer, so they do not contain ice crystals. Rain usually occurs here when some of the larger droplets start to fall under their own weight. These collide with other droplets and get bigger and bigger until eventually they drop right through the cloud base as rain.

Why does it snow?

Snow forms when tiny water droplets freeze into ice crystals, often around microscopic dust particles floating in the air. This usually happens in layer clouds at temperatures of −4°F to −40°F. In very high clouds, such as cirrus, the water freezes into tiny hollow prisms about .02 inches long. In medium-height cloud there is a mixture of solid ice prisms and flat ice plates; and in low cloud there are ice crystals of all shapes and sizes.

The ice crystals are quite heavy, and so start to fall. If the air below the cloud is above 32°F, or freezing point, they melt and fall as rain, but if it is cold enough the crystals will remain frozen. As they fall the crystals collide in the air and often join with others to form star-shaped snowflakes. The biggest flakes and heaviest snowfall occur when the air

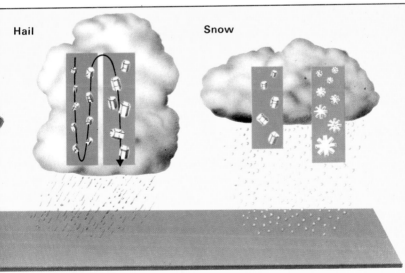

Hail

Snow

▲ **Hailstones are formed in** the turbulent air currents inside storm clouds.

▲ **Snow forms from ice** crystals freezing together, as prisms, plates, or snowflakes.

45

temperature is between 32°F and 35°F. In these conditions, the constant melting and refreezing causes the flakes to grow bigger and bigger as they fall toward the ground.

Rain and snow thus form in the same way: It is the temperature below cloud level that determines which falls. And when the temperature is around 40°F, we get the mixture of rain, snow, and partly melted snowflakes that is known as sleet.

What are hailstones?

In temperate regions we think of hailstones as being like gravel – perhaps up to about 0.2 inches in diameter. In the plains of North America, however, where the most severe storms occur, hailstones are often the size of small birds' eggs. The biggest on record was one measuring 7.5 inches across and weighing 26 ounces which fell in Kansas, in 1970.

Hailstones start off as frozen, or partly frozen, raindrops in tall cumulonimbus clouds. Inside these clouds there are violent upward and downward air currents, moving at speeds of 100 feet a second or more. The frozen raindrops are tossed up and down inside the cloud, and each time they go above freezing level another layer of ice builds up on them, until they become so heavy that they plummet through the cloud base and fall to the ground.

▲ **Snowflakes are all built on** the same six-sided basic plan, but, surprisingly, no two are ever the same.

▲ **The internal structure of a** hailstone consists of numerous layers of ice, rather like the layers of an onion. While the hailstone is being thrown up and down inside a storm cloud, another layer of ice is added to it each time that the hailstone passes above freezing level.

Lightning and Thunder

A blinding white flash of lightning is one of the most violent and unpredictable things in nature. It can split a 500-year-old oak tree from top to bottom in a fraction of a second, or reduce a building to a pile of rubble!

Lightning is an enormous electrical spark caused by a build-up of static electricity in the clouds and on the ground below. When the flash happens, a surge of electrical current of up to 10,000 amps, called a discharge, leaps between the clouds, or between the clouds and the ground.

This huge surge of electrical energy raises the temperature of the air in its path to over 50,000°F – five times as hot as the surface of the Sun! The path of the lightning flash is only a fraction of an inch across, but it is surrounded by a halo of glowing gas several yards across. The air in this thin channel is heated up so quickly by the discharge that it expands violently, sending out a shock wave that we hear as a deafening clap of thunder.

▼ **Storm clouds are lit from** below by the blinding flashes of a lightning storm at night.

What causes lightning?

When raindrops and hailstones are repeatedly swept up and down by the violent air currents within a thundercloud static electricity is generated inside the cloud. It is rather like building up a charge of static electricity on a comb by repeatedly running it through your hair, but on a much larger scale. A large positive charge builds up in the very cold upper parts of the cloud, and a negative charge builds up at the base, which is matched by a buildup of positive charge on the ground below. Eventually, the charges reach a critical level – and the energy in them is released in a blinding flash of lightning.

This kind of discharge, with the spark jumping between the clouds and the ground, is known as forked lightning. But in a thunderstorm there are usually also hundreds of smaller lightning flashes that jump between the clouds. These light up the sky with the flickering blue-white light we call sheet lightning. A third, and much less common kind of lightning, is called ball lightning. This takes the form of a glowing sphere of bright light, about the size of a football, which floats slowly though the air until it fades away, pops like a bubble, or explodes. It is such a curious phenomenon that scientists do not really understand what it is.

LIGHTNING

▼ **A lightning flash is really a** sequence of flashes that usually last about a quarter of a second. First, a leader stroke zigzags toward the ground.

▼ **This is met by a spark** traveling upward. When the two meet they create a path for the main lightning flash, which surges upward from the ground.

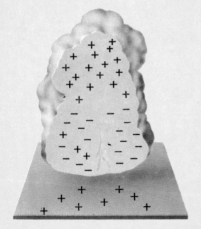

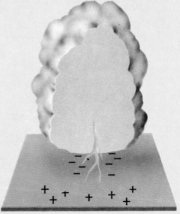

Why do thunderclouds form?

Thunderclouds are much more likely to occur in some climatic regions than in others. Two conditions are necessary for the development of a thundercloud. First, there must be enough moisture in the air for cumulonimbus clouds to form. Second, the air inside the cloud must be unstable, that is, warmer than the surrounding air so that it continues to rise.

Thunderstorms are most frequent in the equatorial regions, where the climate is damp and the intense surface heating causes warm air to rise. Conditions are also ideal in the great central plains of North America.

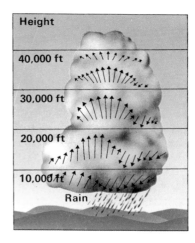

▲ **Air currents inside a big** thundercloud are strong enough to tear a small aircraft apart. The research planes that fly through them are specially strengthened.

▼ **After this, there may be** several more sparks in quick succession – each downward flash followed by a return stroke from ground to cloud.

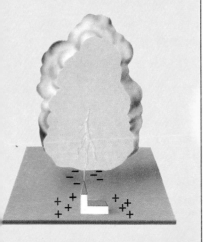

▲ **This is one of only a very** few photographs that have ever been taken of ball lightning. The glowing sphere drifted along the roof of the house for a short time and then simply disappeared.

49

Storms

Of all the weather systems that sweep across the Earth's surface, none can match the power and scale of hurricanes, which sweep across the equatorial oceans, and almost every year bring devastating floods to India and Pakistan during the summer monsoon season.

Hurricanes

These huge circular storm systems are basically the same as the ordinary low pressure weather systems that are carried into the western part of North America from the Pacific and into Europe from the Atlantic, but they are much, much bigger – often more than 400 miles across.

The reason for their great size and power is that they form over tropical seas, where the surface temperature of the ocean is at least 80°F. As the rotating cloud system drifts over the warm water, it picks up huge amounts of moisture and heat energy, feeding off the ocean and growing bigger all the time.

When the storm strikes land, the results can be devastating. Winds of 125 miles an hour or more can flatten plantations, crops, and natural forests, and demolish buildings as if they were sticks of wood.

The top of the hurricane may tower 10 miles above the Earth's surface. Here, the winds spiral outward, drawing out long plumes of ice-crystal cloud.

At ground level, the winds spiral inward. As warm air rises in the cloud, cold air sinks down the central column of low pressure, the eye of the storm.

CHARLESTON, SC

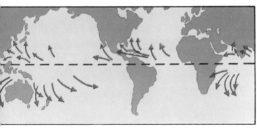

▲ **A satellite view of** the eye of *Hurricane Hugo*, taken on September 21, 1989.

◄ **This map shows** the main tracks of tropical revolving storms.

The hurricane zones

Hurricane is the name given to tropical revolving storms that start in the western Atlantic and sweep across the Caribbean islands or into the southern United States. Similar storms that sweep across the northwest Pacific and into China are called typhoons, while the ones that occur in the Indian Ocean and north of Australia are usually called cyclones.

All are born over the warm seas of the Tropics, usually between 5° and 20° north and south of the Equator. They drift westward at first, then swing away from the Equator and keep going until they strike land, or until they meet colder waters and die out through lack of heat energy.

Tornadoes

Like a hurricane, a tornado is a very rapidly rotating storm with a low pressure zone in its center. But since a tornado is typically around 1,600 feet across, it is much smaller. Its power is concentrated into a narrow column of violently spinning air, with wind speeds often exceeding 125 miles an hour.

The trail of damage left by a tornado is much narrower than that caused by a hurricane, but it is often much more severe. Wind strength alone will often wreck crops and buildings, but there are other hazards too. Violent upward currents of air can pick up animals, people, and trees and dump them some distance away. The eye of the storm contains another deadly menace. Here, the air pressure is so low that if the storm passes right over a house, the sudden drop in air pressure can leave the pressure inside the house much greater than the pressure outside – with the result that the building explodes.

Tornadoes are most common in the Great Plains region of North America. Here, cold, dry air flowing eastward from the Rockies passes over warm, moist air moving northward from the Gulf of Mexico. The combination is very unstable, and violent storms occur many hundreds of times every year.

Monsoons

Big seasonal changes in wind direction and climate take place in many parts of the world, including eastern Asia, the savannas of Africa, and the wooded grasslands of South America. They are called monsoons, from an Arabic word meaning season.

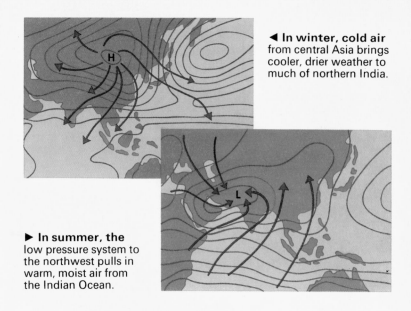

◄ In winter, cold air from central Asia brings cooler, drier weather to much of northern India.

► In summer, the low pressure system to the northwest pulls in warm, moist air from the Indian Ocean.

However, the most dramatic monsoon of all is the one that affects India and the Middle East, because here the whole pattern of air pressure and wind direction is completely reversed twice every year. The changeover is so dramatic that even the currents in the northern part of the Indian Ocean change direction with the twice-yearly change in the winds.

In summer, the vast landmass of Asia is heated by the Sun. Warm air rises over the continent and this creates a low pressure area over northwest India and Pakistan which draws in air from

◄ Traders in Bangkok go about their daily business despite the floods that are a regular feature of the monsoon.

the south. This inflow of air sweeps in over the warm waters of the Indian Ocean, bringing heavy intermittent rains, floods, and quite frequent storms and hurricanes. At this time of year the winds are from the southwest, so this season, from May to September, is often called the Southwest Monsoon.

In winter the pattern is reversed. Asia is dominated by cold air sinking down over the land and flowing outward. This results in the cool dry season of October to April. The high pressure region is farther north this time, in central China, and the strong outflow of air sweeps down from the northeast, right across India and far out into the Indian Ocean.

53

Meteorologists at Work

Meteorology is the scientific study of the atmosphere and the weather systems that occur in its lowermost layers. Some meteorologists make a special study of cloud types. Some examine the ways in which human activities such as agriculture and industry are affecting the atmosphere. And others design computer models to try to predict how the atmosphere will behave in the short-term and far into the future.

Yet to many people, the most familiar meteorologists are the men and women who provide weather forecasts on radio and television. Their work is based on a branch of the science called synoptic meteorology, which is the regular collection, day by day, of millions of pieces of information, from temperature and wind speed, to cloud types, air pressure, and the amount of rain or snow.

Modern weather forecasting depends on a vast network of reporting stations where, every six hours, meteorologists collect this information. It is sent to the forecasting stations, where it is plotted onto charts to show the high and low pressure areas and weather systems.

► **This map shows a typical** weather forecast for Western Europe. A partly occluded front is moving across southwest Britain and northwest France, bringing increased cloud and fresher winds.

Warm front   **Cold front**

Wind

WEATHER SYMBOLS

The wind symbol has a flag which shows wind strength and direction. The shaded area shows amount of cloud cover.

= Mist
≡ Fog
❚ Drizzle
● Rain

✳ Snow
⊻ Rain shower
✴ Snow shower
ℝ Thunderstorm

► **Scientists** regularly send up high-altitude balloons carrying instruments to measure wind speed, air temperature, humidity and pressure, and solar radiation. This nighttime launch was part of a special Swedish project designed to study damage to the ozone layer over the Arctic regions.

Reporting stations

Most of the reporting stations are on the ground, but today the forecasters also receive reports from meteorological aircraft making regular flights, from permanent weather ships, and also from ships traveling over the world's oceans.

One of the most important advances for meteorologists in this century has been the use of satellites. These provide pictures of entire weather systems, and are especially valuable because they cover remote areas of land and sea where there are few ground observers. Satellites, for example, have enabled forecasters to provide warnings of hurricanes forming far out in tropical seas.

The weather in code

Weather information that is transmitted around the world can be read by meteorologists anywhere because every reading and observation is reported in an international code made up of groups of five numbers. The first group of numbers identifies the reporting station, and the report then follows in a set sequence of code groups.

When the information is plotted onto a map, like the one shown opposite, a new set of codes comes into use. This time symbols are used to show the amount of cloud cover, the wind speed and direction, and the main weather features such as rain, fog, thunderstorms, or snow showers. Thin solid lines called isobars join places with the same air pressure, and these lines reveal the pattern of highs and lows that controls the weather. Thicker lines are used to show the position of warm and cold fronts.

The Earth Under Our Feet

About 4,600 million years ago the Earth was a huge, fiery ball of molten rock material, circling the Sun. As the surface layers cooled and formed the Earth's crust, chemical elements in the mixture combined to form minerals. The minerals then joined together in various combinations to make different kinds of rock.

At the same time, the Earth's atmosphere was forming. So almost from the start the rocks of the crust were being worn away by wind and rain and running water.

These forces are still shaping the Earth's surface. We can see them in action all around us. We can also study the composition of the crustal rocks – but the chemistry of the deeper rock layers remains a mystery. The deepest boreholes drilled so far are really little more than pinpricks on the surface since they penetrate only about 5 miles into the Earth's crust.

Most of what we know about the rocks deep inside the Earth comes from studying the lavas and gases that pour from volcanoes, and from investigating the few places on Earth where rocks of the deep layers are pushed up to the surface. Scientists have also learned a lot about the structure of the Earth's interior by studying the way in which earthquake waves are bent and slowed down as they pass through different rock layers.

▶ **The Alps stretch over** 600 miles in an arc across southern Europe, from southern France in the west to Austria in the east. The range was formed more than ten million years ago by Africa pushing north against Europe.

The Structure of the Earth

As the Earth was cooling, the molten rock material began to separate into different layers. When a pan of jam is boiling on a stove, a light frothy "scum" forms on the surface. Something very similar to this happened during the first billion years of the Earth's life. The lighter minerals in the molten mixture floated upward and became concentrated in the surface layers, while the heavier minerals sank and became concentrated nearer the center.

The crust

The outermost layer of the Earth is called the crust. It is very thin compared with the Earth's diameter – about 25 miles thick under the continents and even thinner, averaging less than 4 miles, under the oceans.

The very thin crust under the sea consists of dark rock of a type called basalt. Floating on top of this, like huge rafts, are the continents, made mainly of lighter rocks, such as granite.

The mantle

Below the crust lies the mantle. The stiff upper layer of the mantle, together with the crust, form a rocky shell surrounding the Earth called the lithosphere.

The mantle is about 1,700 miles thick and it accounts for nearly 85 percent of the Earth's volume. Near the top, parts of the mantle are molten, and because the rocks there are extremely hot they are in constant, slow motion. It is this movement, deep beneath the Earth's crust, that forces parts of the crust to move around over the surface of the globe.

Most of the mantle, however, is solid, and both its density and its temperature increase with depth. At 1,200 miles beneath the Earth's surface the temperature is about 5,400°F.

The core

The central region of the Earth – the core – begins at a depth of 1,800 miles. It is very dense, and probably consists mainly of iron, and some nickel. The outer part of the core is liquid, but the inner part, about 3,200 miles beneath the Earth's surface, is solid. Here, the temperature is over 9,000°F, and the pressure is enormous – somewhere between 1.3 and 3.5 million times the pressure of the atmosphere at the Earth's surface.

▶ **The interior of the Earth is** divided into four main zones – the crust, the mantle, the outer core, and the inner core – according to the properties of the rocks. Some layers are solid; others are liquid.

THE COMPOSITION OF THE EARTH

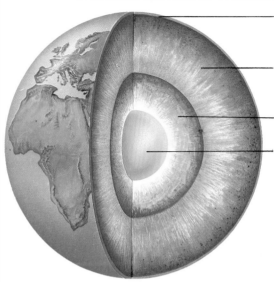

Crust: between 4 and 25 mi thick.

Mantle: about 1,700 mi thick and mainly solid.

Outer core: 1,500 mi thick and molten.

Inner core: Solid, very dense and about 1,500 mi across.

Peridotite

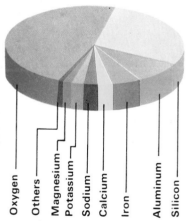

Oxygen
Others
Magnesium
Potassium
Sodium
Calcium
Iron
Aluminum
Silicon

▲ **The Earth's mantle may** be composed in part of a dark rock called peridotite.

▲ **This pie-chart shows** the main elements that make up the Earth's crust.

PLANET EARTH FACTS

Age: 4,600,000,000 years

Diameter from pole to pole through the Earth's center: 7,882 mi

Circumference through both poles: 24,859.82 mi

Total volume: 260,052,000,000 mi³

Total surface area: 196,860,000 mi²

Land surface area: 57,514,000 mi²

Land as percentage of surface: 29.2%

Water surface area: 139,346,000 mi²

Water as percentage of surface: 70.8%

Average height of land above sea level: 2,755 feet

Average depth of oceans: 12,490 feet

Rocks and Landscapes

Looking at a landscape can be fascinating. There in front of you lies a whole range of clues that can tell you such things as: what kind of rocks the scenery is made of and what has happened to them since they were formed, and how old the landscape is and what processes have shaped it.

Some landscapes are very young. The Alps, for example, have not been around for very long in geological terms. They are still extremely high, with steep rock faces, razor-sharp ridges and pointed peaks. Their sharp, jagged features reflect the rock-shattering effect of the freezing cold and the gouging effect of moving masses of ice, called glaciers.

Compare that scene with the hills of Scotland. This is a much older landscape. It, too, was carved by frost and glaciers, and once was a world of sharp peaks and ridges. But here, millions of years of erosion have worn away the sharpness, leaving a much smoother, more rounded landscape. Far in the future, this is what the Alps will look like.

▼ **Ropy lava has poured from** a volcano in the Galápagos Islands and then solidified, forming this striking landscape.

Rock types

Rocks can be divided into three families according to the way in which they were formed. There are igneous rocks, sedimentary rocks, and metamorphic rocks.

Igneous rocks

The word igneous comes from the Latin word *igneus,* which means "fire." It is a general name used for the large and varied family of rock types that start off as molten rock, or magma, beneath the Earth's crust. These rocks are all made up of minerals whose crystals are tightly locked together.

Some igneous rocks are formed deep in the crust, where molten magma is forced into cavities or cracks in the rock layers and then hardens. These are called intrusive rocks. Mil-

▲ **Le Puy in France is the** solidified central plug of an old volcano. The layers of lava that surrounded it and formed the volcanic cone have long since been worn away.

▲ **A section through a volcanic** landscape shows a large underground chamber (1), from which molten magma rises up the volcano's central vent (2). During eruptions, ash (3) may be shot into the air, and lava (4) may pour out of the vent. The magma that cools down underground forms sills (5) when it hardens between

lions of years later, if the overlying rocks are worn away, intrusive rocks may become exposed at the surface.

Since the magma that hardens into intrusive rocks is inside the Earth, it cools down slowly. The result is that the individual crystals in the new rocks are often quite large. For example, in granite, which is one of the most common igneous rocks, the main crystals – feldspar, quartz, and mica – are easily seen with the naked eye. In some varieties the individual crystals are a third of an inch or more across.

Rocks formed on the Earth's surface are called extrusive rocks. They usually occur when the magma that pours from volcanoes (which is known as lava)

cools down. The ash that is emitted from volcanoes is made up of tiny pieces of lava. When this ash solidifies it forms extrusive rocks known as tuffs.

The lava that forms extrusive rocks is exposed to the air so it cools down quickly, and as a result the crystals in the new rock are very small. In many types of extrusive rock the crystals that make up the rock can be seen and identified only by using a special geological microscope.

rock layers, and dikes (6) when it hardens across rock layers. Laccoliths (7) are formed when the intrusive mass of magma pushes up the overlying rocks.

IGNEOUS ROCKS

1. Basalt
2. Rhyolite
3. Syenite
4. Obsidian
5. Scandinavian granite
6. Ignimbrite

▲ **Basalt is the most common** extrusive rock. It forms from the fluid lava that pours out of the volcano, often covering large areas. Rhyolite forms from thicker, more sluggish lava. Its crystals are too small to see. Obsidian has the same composition as rhyolite. It cools so quickly that it forms volcanic glass with no visible crystals. Ignimbrite is made from the pieces of ash that erupt from volcanoes. When the ash settles it is still so hot that it welds together to make a very hard rock.

Granite is found in almost all intrusive rock formations. It is usually a mottled shade of white, gray, pink, or red. Since it is a very hard rock, granite may often resist erosion. Syenite is a coarse-grained rock that is similar to granite but much less common.

Sedimentary rocks

As soon as a rock is exposed at the Earth's surface, wind, rain, frost, and ice start to wear it away. This process is called erosion. The fine rock debris that is worn away is carried downhill and dumped in lowland areas or in the sea. There it forms thick layers of sand, silt, or mud, called sediments, which slowly become buried as more sediment is dumped on top.

Millions of years later the soft sediments have been changed into solid rock by the huge pressure of the overlying sediments, and by chemical changes that take place in the sediments themselves.

The main types of sedimentary rock are sandstones, silts, and mudstones. Most of these have grains that are fairly evenly sized. However, some sedimentary rocks consist of large rounded pebbles set in a mass of sand and cemented together with the minerals calcite or silica. These are called conglomerates or pudding stones and they are the remains of old riverbeds or beaches.

Some sedimentary rocks have a very different history. Limestone, for example, consists mainly of calcite, which is often made from the shells of tiny sea creatures that have died and sunk to the seabed. Some limestones are the

▼ **Most sedimentary rocks** are laid down in flat, horizontal layers called beds or strata. Here, beds of the soft rock shale are being worn away faster than the harder limestone layers.

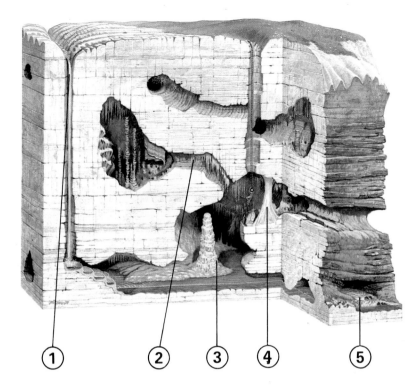

remains of ancient coral reefs and are full of fossils (see page 86). Other types of limestone are formed chemically, when calcite particles in sea water combine with sand grains. The result is a mass of tiny rounded grains, each about 0.04 inch across, that are then cemented together into a solid rock.

Sedimentary landscapes
One of the most noticeable things about sedimentary rocks is that they are nearly always built up in layers, and these are often clearly visible in cliffs, quarries, and riverbanks. In each

▲ **A section through limestone** country shows the caves and tunnels formed by rainwater. Streams enter caves at the surface (1) and emerge near the base (5). Inside the caves stalactites (2), stalagmites (3), and columns (4) may be formed as dissolved limestone is deposited by the dripping water.

case, the older rocks are at the bottom and the younger ones are higher up; unless, that is, the rocks have been turned upside down by earth movements (see pages 78–79). Geologists can examine the grain size in order to tell if the rock is the right way up or if it has been overturned.

Sandstones vary a great deal in hardness, so different layers will be eroded at different rates, often resulting in dramatic landscapes. Typical sandstone country may be rolling hills or high, bleak moors with steep, rocky crags.

Limestone scenery is easy to recognize. Quite apart from the pale color of the rock, the landscape is often dotted with streams that suddenly vanish down holes. This is because the small amount of acid that occurs naturally in rainwater dissolves limestone. Below ground the rainwater creates a maze of potholes and caves, often containing spectacular limestone pillars called stalactites and stalagmites.

▲ This sandstone pillar was sandblasted into shape by the desert wind.

▼ Reef limestone consists of the remains of ancient coral reefs. Devonian sandstone was formed in desert conditions millions of years ago. Chalk is made of the shells of tiny sea-living organisms.

SEDIMENTARY ROCKS

1. Reef limestone
2. Devonian sandstone
3. Chalk

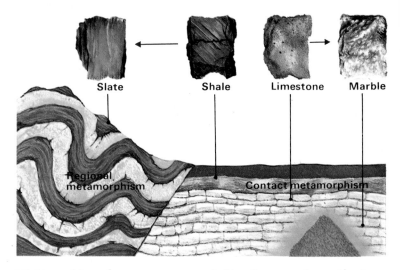

Slate Shale Limestone Marble

Regional metamorphism Contact metamorphism

Metamorphic rocks

The third family of rock types consists of metamorphic rocks. The word metamorphic comes from the Greek *metamorphosis*, meaning "to change," and this family consists of rocks that started off as igneous or sedimentary rocks but were then changed. The alteration can be caused either by the intense pressure of earth movements squeezing and folding the rock layers (see pages 78–79), or by intense heat if the rock layers come into contact with hot igneous rocks.

▶ 1. Marble: The white marble shown here comes from Carrara, Italy. There are also black, green, red, and yellow varieties.
2. Slate: a fine-grained rock. During metamorphism the crystals of the iron minerals in slate may grow so that they are easily visible, as in this picture.

▲ The diagram shows the two main kinds of metamorphism, regional and contact, plus two metamorphic changes – shale into slate and limestone into marble.

Metamorphism caused by large-scale earth movements is called regional metamorphism, and it can affect rocks over many hundreds of miles. By contrast, contact metamorphism only af-

METAMORPHIC ROCKS

1

fects the rocks close to the source of the heat.

One of the most familiar types of metamorphic rock is slate. This dark, smooth rock is hard and brittle and it splits very easily into thin sheets. This makes it ideal for covering roofs. It is formed when shale or mudstone is altered by pressure during earth movements. Another very fam-

2 — Crystals

▲ **The Carrara marble quarry** in Italy produces some of the world's finest stone. It was used by Michelangelo for many of his most famous sculptures.

iliar type is marble, often used as a decorative stone in banks, hotels, and other important buildings. It is easily cut and can be highly polished. Marble is produced when limestone is altered by the heat of a lava flow or by contact with molten rocks far below the ground.

Most metamorphic rocks are quite hard and resistant to the forces of erosion, and so they often form areas of high ground. The Highland region of Scotland, for example, contains a great variety of metamorphic rocks, including many types of schist (originally mudstones and shales) and gneiss (which may have originally been either igneous or sedimentary rocks).

69

The Rock Cycle

The weathering processes that eat away at rocks on the Earth's surface; the winds, rivers, and glaciers that carry the rock debris down to the sea; and the methods by which the rock dust is piled into dunes or mud banks, all form part of a continuous cycle. Yet the part we can see is only half the story.

Once the sediments have been deposited a new part of the rock cycle begins. Slowly, very slowly, the water is squeezed out of them. They are crushed deeper and deeper into the Earth where heat and pressure alter them. Their minerals are remixed. New ones are added. And finally, large-scale earth movements force the new rocks back up to the surface and the cycle starts all over again.

1. Rain, wind, ice, and frost gradually break rocks down into fragments.

2. Winds, rivers, and glaciers pick up the debris and sweep it away.

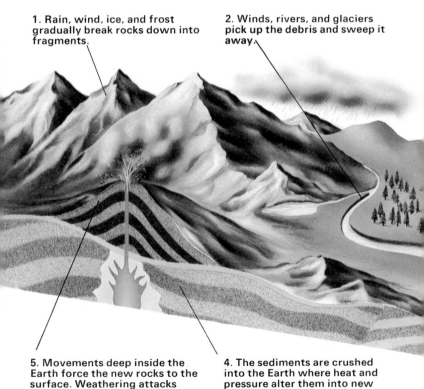

5. Movements deep inside the Earth force the new rocks to the surface. Weathering attacks them and the cycle begins again.

4. The sediments are crushed into the Earth where heat and pressure alter them into new kinds of rock.

MOUNTAIN HEIGHTS

	Feet
Everest, Tibet/Nepal:	29,028
K2, Kashmir/Sinkiang:	28,250
Kanchenjunga, Nepal/Sikkim:	28,208
Makalu, Tibet/Nepal:	27,824
Dhaulagiri, Nepal:	26,810
Nanga Parbat, Jammu/Kashmir:	26,660
Annapurna, Nepal:	26,504
Gasherbrum, Kashmir:	26,470
Gosainthan (Xixabangma Feng), Tibet:	26,287
Nanda Devi, India:	25,645
Rakaposhi, Jammu/Kashmir:	25,550
Kamet, India/Tibet:	25,447
Namcha Barwa, Tibet:	25,445
Gurla Mandhata, Tibet:	25,355
Ulugh Muztagh, Tibet/Sinkiang:	25,340
Kungur (Kongur Shan), Sinkiang:	25,325
Tirich Mir, Pakistan:	25,230

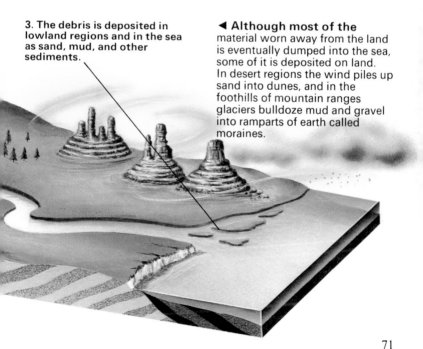

3. The debris is deposited in lowland regions and in the sea as sand, mud, and other sediments.

◀ Although most of the material worn away from the land is eventually dumped into the sea, some of it is deposited on land. In desert regions the wind piles up sand into dunes, and in the foothills of mountain ranges glaciers bulldoze mud and gravel into ramparts of earth called moraines.

Earth's Changing Face

The continents and oceans form a familiar pattern over the surface of the Earth. We know it well from atlases and, in recent years, from photographs taken from spacecraft. But the world has not always looked like this.

Between about 500 million years ago and 300 million years ago there were just three big continents, moving slowly over the surface of the globe. About 275 million years ago they collided, and stuck together forming one huge supercontinent called Pangaea. But that too eventually cracked and split apart. The fragments drifted into the positions we see them in today – and they are still on the move. The Atlantic Ocean is getting wider by an inch or more a year, the Pacific Ocean is getting smaller, and the Red Sea is part of a huge crack in the Earth's crust that will widen to produce a new ocean millions of years in the future.

The idea that the continents have moved is not new. Evidence that they had once been joined together has been around for many years, but no one could explain how or why sections of the

▼ Telltale fossils show clearly that the continents were once joined. For example, fossils of the plant *Glossopteris* and the animals *Mesosaurus* and *Lystrosaurus* have all been found in the southern continents which are now widely separated.

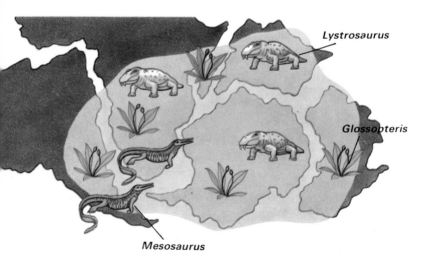

Lystrosaurus

Glossopteris

Mesosaurus

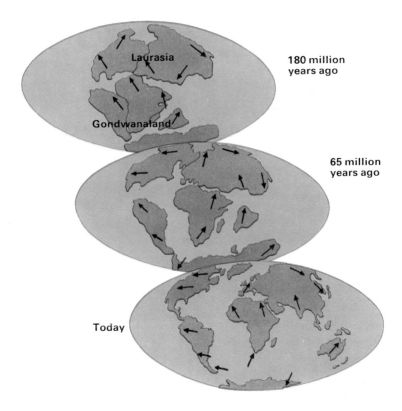

▲ **Three maps showing the**
slow movement of the continents.

Earth's crust could possibly have moved over the surface of the globe. The breakthrough came in the early 1960s when ocean scientists discovered that the thin, rocky plates of the Earth's outer crust were being carried along by slow-moving currents in the semi-liquid rocks of the mantle below.

The wandering continents

About 180 million years ago the supercontinent of Pangaea began to split into two. The northern part is known as Laurasia and the southern part as Gondwanaland.

As the two great continents drifted northward 135 million years ago, Gondwanaland was already breaking up. India had separated and was making its own way north, while Australia and Antarctica were still locked together. Africa and South America were starting to separate.

Sixty-five million years ago the world was starting to take on a much more familiar look. The widening South Atlantic Ocean had separated Africa and South America, and Madagascar had

73

broken away from Africa. Only the two great southern landmasses, Australia and Antarctica, remained joined.

The final act that shaped the modern world occurred when India collided with Asia, bulldozing the rocks of the Earth's crust 5 miles into the air to form the mountain range we now call the Himalayas.

Plate tectonics

Ocean surveys in the 1960s revealed a network of mountain ridges running down the middle of the main ocean basins, and deep trenches in the seabed running along the edges of many of

▼ **The Earth's crust is made** up of eight large main plates and several smaller plates.

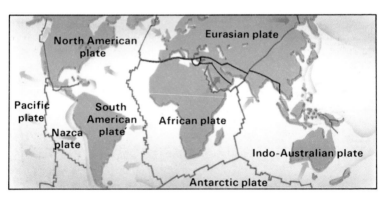

The ocean ridge has deep cracks along the center where magma rises to the surface.

Faults, or breaks, crossing the ridge allow sections of crust to move past each other.

The molten rock forms new ocean crust which moves outward from the ridge.

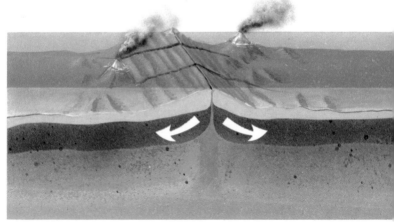

the continents. These ridges and trenches mark the edges of a number of large sections of the Earth's crust called plates. These plates are all in motion.

There are deep cracks in the crust along the center of the ocean ridges, and through these cracks molten rock from the mantle below is forcing its way to the surface. When it reaches the surface the rock hardens to form new ocean crust, which is then forced to spread outward from the ridge to make way for more molten rock pushing up from below. The result is that the seabed is spreading outward from the ridges like a series of huge conveyor belts.

The Earth, however, is not getting bigger. To compensate for new crust being formed at the ridges, old crust must be destroyed somewhere else – and that explains the presence of the trenches. Here, the front edges of moving plates are being forced down beneath the edges of other plates. The crustal rocks melt as they are pushed down into the mantle, and they also grind and jolt as they are forced past each other. These regions are called subduction zones, and it is no coincidence that subduction zones are also the world's main earthquake and volcano zones. The edges of the Pacific Ocean are ringed by subduction trenches, and earthquakes and eruptions are so common here that this region has been called the Ring of Fire.

▼ **The diagram below shows** how new crust is formed at the mid-ocean ridge while older crust is destroyed at a subduction zone.

The expanding crust is forced down beneath another plate in the subduction zone.

As the two plates are forced against each other, rock layers are crushed and folded.

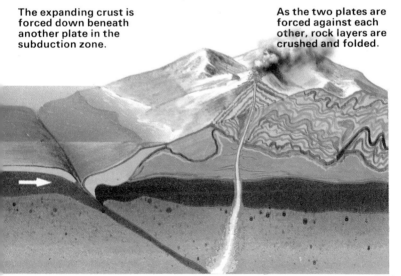

▲ The Tonga Trench has formed where the Australian and Pacific plates meet. Melting of the descending plate has produced an arc of volcanic islands.

▼ The Peru-Chile Trench marks where the Nazca plate plunges under South America, forcing up the Andes mountains.

Island hot spots

Take a close look at a map of the Pacific Ocean and it soon becomes clear that the Hawaiian Islands, Caroline Islands, Society Islands, and many other island groups are not just scattered about at random: They occur in almost straight lines. What's more, the islands are all volcanic in origin, and those at one end of the chain are always much younger than those at the other end. Seafarers have known this for centuries, but none of it could be explained until scientists came up with the theory of plate tectonics.

The explanation is that the islands form over hot spots in the mantle, which are small,

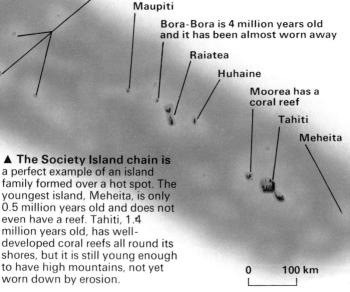

Atolls de l'Ouest. All the islands beyond Bora-Bora are now just atolls.

Maupiti

Bora-Bora is 4 million years old and it has been almost worn away

Raiatea

Huhaine

Moorea has a coral reef

Tahiti

Meheita

▲ The Society Island chain is a perfect example of an island family formed over a hot spot. The youngest island, Meheita, is only 0.5 million years old and does not even have a reef. Tahiti, 1.4 million years old, has well-developed coral reefs all round its shores, but it is still young enough to have high mountains, not yet worn down by erosion.

0   100 km

localized areas of intense volcanic activity. As the crustal plate drifts over the hot spot, magma forces its way up and an island is formed. It is then carried onward, away from the hot spot, and a new island begins to form over the original spot.

The first island is carried farther and farther away by the moving plate. The eruptions stop and the forces of erosion start to wear down the island's steep sides. In the Tropics a coral reef forms around the island and, as the island continues to shrink, the corals grow upward. Finally, the island sinks below sea level and all that is visible is a coral reef surrounding a shallow lagoon. The reef is now called an atoll.

▲ **A typical volcanic island in** French Polynesia. The island is getting lower and lower as its steep slopes are worn away. At the same time a wide reef is growing round the island.

Living rocks
Coral reefs are built by tiny creatures called polyps. Each animal builds a tiny cup of calcium carbonate in which to live, and when it dies the next generation builds on top. After thousands of years the living colony can produce a massive reef of limestone – dead rock inside, but with a thin surface layer of living animals. The Great Barrier Reef of Australia is a chain of coral reefs and islands that stretches for more than 1,200 miles.

Rocks Under Pressure

The geological forces that move whole sections of the Earth's crust over the surface of the globe operate very slowly, but they are immensely powerful. They can wipe out entire ocean basins, raise mountain ranges, and split continents apart. The Red Sea and the great rift valleys of East Africa, for example, are all part of a vast system of cracks in the crust that will one day split Africa apart and give birth to a new ocean.

Even smaller localized forces can produce spectacular results. Wherever there are cliffs or mountains, the exposed rock faces reveal faults and folds of all shapes and sizes where the rocks have been crushed or stretched, or even turned upside down.

Folding and faulting

Although we use the expression "as solid as a rock" for something that cannot move, rocks are not as rigid as they seem. When horizontal layers are squeezed by earth movements they buckle and bend, just like modeling clay. If the pressure is fairly gentle and steady over a long period of time, the rocks will buckle into

▼ **Folds occur when rock** layers are squeezed, so they are common in regions where plates have collided, forcing the rocks to buckle into mountain ranges.

▼ **Faults occur where the** Earth's crust is being stretched or compressed so violently that the rock layers break in a horizontal or vertical movement.

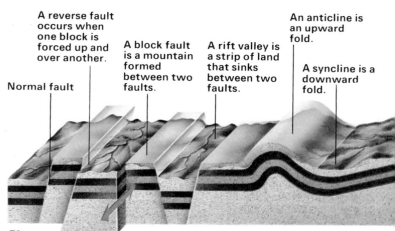

A reverse fault occurs when one block is forced up and over another.

Normal fault

A block fault is a mountain formed between two faults.

A rift valley is a strip of land that sinks between two faults.

An anticline is an upward fold.

A syncline is a downward fold.

▲ **Sandstone and shale beds** in this cliff have been crushed into concertina folds and then stood on end by a series of ancient earth movements.

Overturned fold

A nappe and thrust fault occurs if the top section of rock slides over the lower one.

smooth, regular waves, called folds. If the pressure is more sudden or severe, the whole fold may be overturned so that the rock layers end up completely upside down. If the pressure continues, the fold may even tear apart so that the upper section of rock slides gradually over the lower one.

Faults are actual breaks in the rock layers, and they can be caused either by squeezing or by stretching of the crust. The smallest are tiny cracks that occur in mineral crystals. The largest produce huge landscape features, such as the Great Glen fault in Scotland and the 3,000-mile-long East African Rift Valley.

Earthquakes

The plates of the Earth's crust may move an inch or so in a year, but the forces involved are colossal. Where plates are moving away from each other the movement does not create a problem. However, in regions where plates are sliding past each other, or where one plate is being forced down beneath another, the stresses on the rocks are enormous. The plates can become jammed against each other, and the stresses build up until something has to give. What happens then is the most dramatic and frightening of all natural events – an earthquake.

This occurs when the two plates that were jammed together suddenly slip past each other, perhaps for a distance of several yards, releasing violent shock waves that can often be detected on the opposite side of the Earth.

Huge areas can be completely devastated. Buildings collapse as the ground ripples and heaves. Roads, bridges, and railway lines are broken and twisted. Water mains, gas pipes, electricity lines, and sewers are destroyed – adding fire and disease to the

▼ Most earthquakes are caused by rock movements along faults at depths of 6–18 mi, although some occur as deep as 400 mi.

The epicenter is the point on the surface immediately above the focus.

Shock waves travel outward through the rock layers.

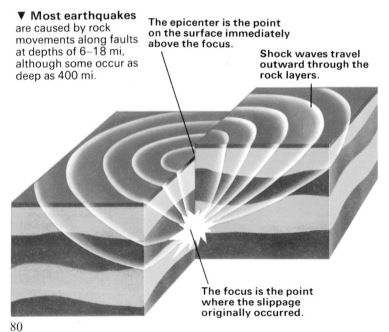

The focus is the point where the slippage originally occurred.

▲ **The destruction caused by** an earthquake in Sicily in 1968.

dangers already facing the rescuers, the injured, and those left without homes.

These shock waves can be recorded by an instrument called a seismograph. Scientists use the recorded information to discover the location and intensity of earthquakes. The strength of an earthquake is measured on a scale of numbers from one to ten called the Richter scale. Earthquakes measuring more than seven on this scale usually cause immense damage and claim many lives.

"X-raying" the Earth

Much of what we know about the Earth's interior layers was revealed by the study of earthquake shock waves. There are

TSUNAMIS

When earthquakes happen beneath the sea they often create enormous sea waves called tsunamis. These can spread outward at up to 500 mi/h, rearing 130 ft high as they hit shallow coastal waters and surge inland, where they cause vast amounts of damage.

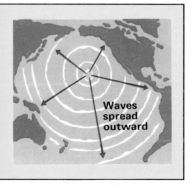

Waves spread outward

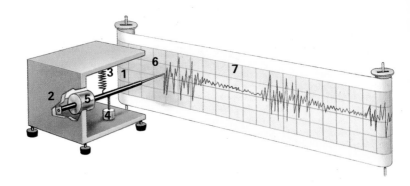

three main kinds. Primary waves (P) will pass through solids and liquids and therefore can pass through the Earth's core. They bend as they pass between layers of different density (just as light rays are bent when passing from air to water, making a drinking straw appear bent at the water surface). The bending of these waves creates an area on the Earth's surface where no P waves are detected. This is called a shadow zone.

The secondary waves (S) do not pass through liquids at all, so at the boundary between the mantle and the core they are reflected back toward the Earth's surface. This creates a shadow zone at the surface where S waves are not felt. The pattern of shadow zones revealed that the Earth had two contrasting core regions – an outer fluid core and a very dense, solid inner core.

The third kind of waves are long waves (L). These travel slowly through the Earth's surface layers and they are the ones that cause the damage.

▲ **The seismograph consists** of an arm (1) hinged at one end (2) and controlled by a spring (3) and damper (4). When the Earth trembles, the weight (5) remains almost still while the rest of the instrument shakes, causing the pen (6) to leave a trace on the moving chart (7).

▼ **Although P and S waves can** travel great distances through the Earth, it is the very much slower L waves, traveling only along the surface, that do the damage.

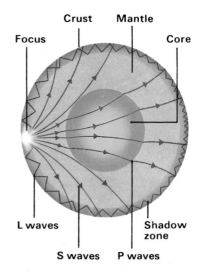

Crust Mantle
Focus Core
L waves Shadow zone
S waves P waves

Geophysical Prospecting

The study of the Earth in search of raw materials such as minerals and fuels is called geophysical prospecting. Minerals include metals such as iron, copper, and lead, and nonmetals such as sulfur and salt. They are used by manufacturing industries. The fossil fuels oil, coal, and gas provide much of the energy we use. They were formed from the remains of plants and animals and so they can be buried very deep inside the Earth. Geologists study the structure of the Earth in order to find these hidden riches.

Prospecting for minerals

The rocks of the Earth's crust contain hundreds of different minerals. Most minerals are mixtures of chemical elements. The metals that are so important to industry, for example, are found as mixtures called ores. The ores are mined and then crushed, so that the metal can be extracted.

Two common methods of mineral prospecting involve measuring the pull of gravity

▼ An offshore rig drills for oil in the North Sea.

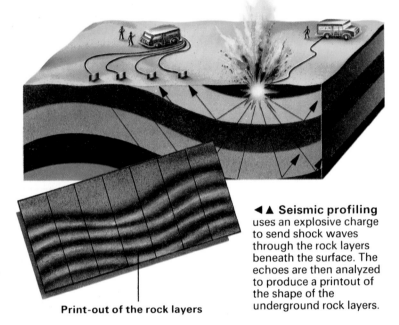

Print-out of the rock layers

◀▲ **Seismic profiling** uses an explosive charge to send shock waves through the rock layers beneath the surface. The echoes are then analyzed to produce a printout of the shape of the underground rock layers.

and measuring the magnetic field around the Earth. Gravity surveys measure gravity at various points. If there are dense rocks such as mineral ores below, the reading will be high. If there is a large mass of rock salt below, then the meter will give a low reading.

Magnetometers are often towed behind aircraft in order to survey large areas quickly. The equipment takes continuous readings of the Earth's magnetic field. A sudden increase in the reading will indicate the presence of magnetic rocks like iron ores.

Prospecting for oil and gas

The study of earthquakes has revealed that vibrations and shock waves travel easily through solid materials. This fact has led to one of the most important methods of prospecting for oil and gas. It is called seismic profiling and it consists of creating a small earthquake by setting off an explosive charge in a shallow borehole.

Shock waves are released by this explosion. The echoes that

Anticline trap

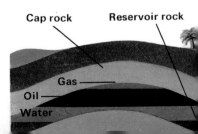

Cap rock   Reservoir rock

Gas

Oil

Water

bounce back from the rock layers below are picked up by lines of special microphones laid out on the ground, which record the echoes on magnetic tape for analysis later. The result is a very accurate picture of the shape and thickness of the deep rock layers. From this, geologists can pick out rock structures where it is likely that oil may be trapped.

▲ **A geologist sets off an** explosive charge during seismic profiling.

▼ **These are the three main** types of oil and gas traps. In each, oil and gas seep upward through porous rocks until they are stopped by a rock they cannot pass through. This is known as the cap rock. The oil and gas collect below this in the reservoir rock.

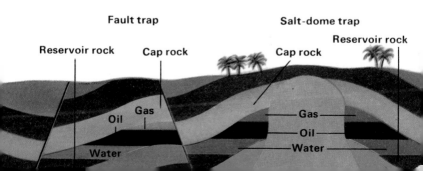

Fault trap

Salt-dome trap

Reservoir rock

Cap rock

Cap rock

Reservoir rock

Oil

Gas

Gas

Oil

Water

Water

Fossils

Fossils are traces of animals or plants that have been preserved in rocks. Most are found in the sediments of ancient seas, lakes, and rivers. The reason for this is quite simple. For a fossil to form, the dead animal must be buried very quickly in sediment, otherwise it will rot away or be eaten by scavengers. Even so, the soft parts of most animals do not survive as fossils; usually only the hard parts, their shells, bones, and teeth, are preserved.

Fossils may be formed in several different ways. Minerals in the water may seep into the tiny spaces in a shell or bone and fill them up. In another process, the shell or bone slowly dissolves away, and is replaced, atom by atom, by the mineral. This gives a perfect mineral replica of the original. Less well preserved fossils form when a shell, trapped in a layer of sediment, dissolves away leaving a space. This is then filled up with minerals or very fine sediment, so that a "cast" is formed of the animal's shape.

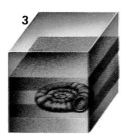

▲ **This ammonite** died (1) and sank to the seabed (2) where the soft parts soon rotted away. Once the shell was buried (3) the original shell dissolved away and was replaced by minerals in the water (4). The result is a well-preserved fossil (5).

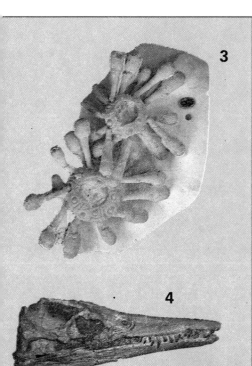

◄ **Fossils can tell us** a great deal about how life evolved. *Trigonia* (1) is one of many kinds of shellfish that lived 65–230 million years ago. Trilobites (2) are even older. They were most abundant 450–500 million years ago.

Other sea creatures include sea urchins (3) and fish-eating ichthyosaurs (4). The leaves of ferns (5) may be preserved in fine sediments, but the most perfect specimens of all are insects caught in amber (6) – the resin that seeped from ancient tree trunks.

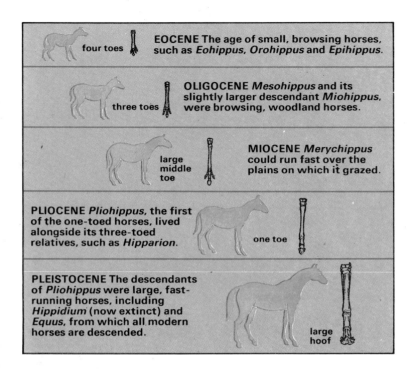

EOCENE The age of small, browsing horses, such as *Eohippus*, *Orohippus* and *Epihippus*.

four toes

OLIGOCENE *Mesohippus* and its slightly larger descendant *Miohippus*, were browsing, woodland horses.

three toes

MIOCENE *Merychippus* could run fast over the plains on which it grazed.

large middle toe

PLIOCENE *Pliohippus*, the first of the one-toed horses, lived alongside its three-toed relatives, such as *Hipparion*.

one toe

PLEISTOCENE The descendants of *Pliohippus* were large, fast-running horses, including *Hippidium* (now extinct) and *Equus*, from which all modern horses are descended.

large hoof

Clues to the past

Fossils are fascinating and beautiful objects in their own right, which is why they are often used as paperweights, ornaments, and brooches. But there is very much more to a good fossil than mere decoration.

By studying fossils from rocks of different ages it is possible to see how one animal or plant has evolved, or developed, from an earlier type that was similar but not exactly the same. These small changes, which occurred for generation after generation, can help us trace the path of evolution from the earliest animals and plants to those we know today.

▲ The evolution of the modern horse has been traced back 55 million years to a tiny forest animal about 1 ft high at the shoulder. Over the years the horse's feet and teeth, and its size, have changed to suit the animal for life on open plains.

The record is far from being complete. There are still a great many "missing links." Yet despite the gaps in the story, enough plant and animal fossils have been found for geologists to build up a remarkably clear idea of what the Earth was like at various times in the past. It is the careful research work of many hundreds of paleontologists around the world that now makes it possible for museums to create lifelike scenes from the distant past.

Telltale indicators

In the distant past, some groups of animals and plants changed much more quickly than others, so that each variety was around for only a relatively short time. These fossils are very useful. They are called zone fossils or indicator fossils and they can be dated very accurately. This means that whenever a geologist finds one in a layer of rock, he knows that rock is exactly the same age as every other rock that contains the same fossil, even if the rocks are many hundreds of miles apart. This accurate dating of rock layers is extremely valuable in making maps of the Earth's crust.

Petroleum geologists study rock samples taken from boreholes that go deep into the Earth's crust. They use the tiny fossils of marine animals as indicators of certain rock types where it is possible that oil may be found. The most likely place to find oil is in a series of rocks containing thick seabed shales, porous sandstone or limestone, and a nonporous rock such as clay. Oil and gas form from the animal and plant remains trapped in the mud and shale. The porous layers higher up act as a storage reservoir, and the nonporous rock forms a lid to stop the oil and gas from leaking away.

▼ **Fossil animal and plant remains** have enabled paleontologists to reconstruct the past.

The Oceans

For most of human history the ocean depths remained unstudied, waiting for the right technology to come along. Tides and currents were used by seafarers far back in the distant past, although what caused them was unknown. Nevertheless, people traveled by raft or primitive boat from southern Asia to Australia more than 40,000 years ago, and 5,000 years ago trading ships sailed between the cities of the Mediterranean.

In the fourth century B.C. the Greek scientist Aristotle wrote about the salt content of the Mediterranean Sea, and about its animal and plant life, but what went on deep beneath the surface remained shrouded in mystery. It was not until almost 2,000 years later that the modern scientific study of the oceans, known as oceanography, began.

The first real oceanographic expedition was the four-year, round-the-world voyage of HMS *Challenger*, which began in 1872. During the voyage, depths were measured with a weighted line wherever the sea was shallow enough, samples were taken of seabed deposits, and thousands of specimens of marine life were caught in nets and dredges.

Today, oceanographers are armed with a huge array of high-technology equipment and they are still discovering more about the ocean depths.

▶ **A wave rears up and spills** over as it approaches the beach – perhaps having started life on the edge of a storm hundreds of miles away, out in the open ocean.

The Ocean Basins

The deep ocean floor lies at an average depth of about 12,000 feet below sea level. Between this dark submarine world and the dry land of the continents lie the continental shelf and the continental slope. The continental shelf is covered by sea but is really part of the land. It is the submerged outer edge of a continent and it slopes gently downward to about 460 feet below sea level. Then there is a sudden change of slope: From the edge of the continental shelf the seabed plunges downward much more steeply, until the ocean floor is reached. This is the continental slope and it is the boundary between the continents and the deep ocean basins.

It would be wrong, however, to think of the ocean floor as a flat, unbroken expanse of mud or sand. Some parts are flat, but snaking down the center of the Atlantic Ocean, and through the Indian, Southern, and Pacific Oceans, are huge mountain ranges. These are called mid-ocean ridges.

Mid-ocean ridges

The discovery of the mid-ocean ridges in the 1960s finally solved the mystery of how the continents had moved over the face of the globe. Huge, steep-sided rift valleys were found running all the way along the center of the ridges, and matching bands of rock on opposite sides of the ridges were found to have exactly the same age, thickness, composition, and magnetism. They could only be such a perfect match if they had formed in the same place, at the same time. After more research, the scientists solved the puzzle. About 2.2 miles below the ocean waves, molten rock was welling up through the central rift valleys and spreading out at either side. The deep seabed was acting just like a vast system of paired conveyor belts.

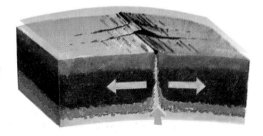

► **The crustal plates** move apart as molten rock pushes its way up from the mantle and solidifies onto the edge of each plate.

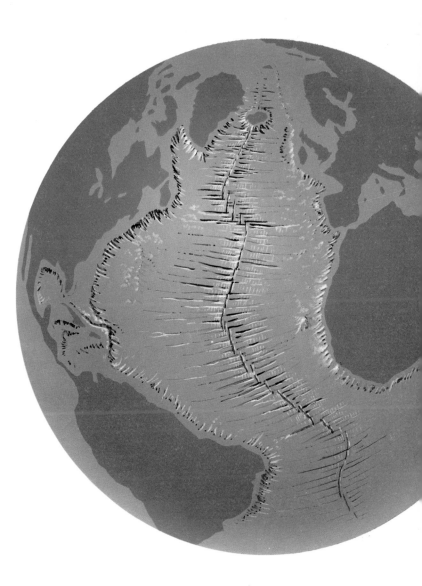

▲ The floor of the Atlantic
Ocean is dominated by a mid-ocean ridge. This is up to 16,000 ft high in places and up to 13,000 ft wide. It is broken into short sections by hundreds of faults that run across it. The central rift valley is 15–30 mi wide, with very steep sides formed by faults that are almost vertical.

93

▲ The Red Sea is a fairly young crack in the Earth's crust. It is 200 mi across at its widest point. Yet if it continues to widen at its present rate, in 200 million years it could be as wide as the Atlantic Ocean is today.

▼ The Pacific Ocean is getting smaller as old crust is swallowed up in the trenches around its edges.

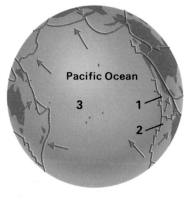

Pacific Ocean

3   1

2

The Pacific Ocean

Over 100 million years ago the Pacific Ocean was a good deal bigger than it is today. At that time there were four main crustal plates, moving outward from mid-ocean ridges and being swallowed at ocean trenches. By 30 million years ago the northern-most plate had disappeared completely, apart from one small fragment which is still there today. At the same time, a large plate in the eastern part of the Pacific Ocean split into several smaller plates. Two of them, the Cocos Plate and the Nazca Plate, survive today off the west coast of Central and South America.

KEY TO MAP
1. Cocos Plate
2. Nazca Plate
3. Pacific Plate

Exploring the Oceans

Some of the equipment used to collect samples of seabed sediments, deep-sea water, and marine life is very similar to equipment that was used 100 years ago. Water samples, for example, are still collected with bottles. These are lowered down to the required depth. A weight, called a messenger, is then slid down the wire. When it strikes the release mechanism the bottle swings upside-down and its valves close, trapping a sample of water inside.

Oceanographers, however, also have a host of new methods of gathering information, which may include the use of echo-sounders, pop-up technology, remote-control submersibles, and satellite communication.

Side-scan sonar

Echo-sounding measures the length of time that a pulse of sound takes to echo back from the seabed to a ship. From this, distance can be determined and a picture of the ocean floor can be formed.

▼ A marine scientist (wearing a safety harness) helps launch an instrument package over the side of a research ship.

Side-scan sonar works in the same way, but the sound pulses are sent out sideways so that a much larger area can be covered – up to 18 miles on each side. Signals are sent out from the ship, or from a towed instrument called a "fish." Receivers on the fish then pick up the echoes and the echo pattern is traced onto paper, building up gradually as the ship continues onward, to create a detailed picture of the seabed.

Pop-up technology

The pop-up idea can be used with many different pieces of equipment, such as deep-sea cameras, temperature recorders, and meters that measure ocean currents. The equipment is let

▶ **A manned submersible** studies the ocean basin. A recent development are small, remote-operated vehicles (ROVs) that are useful for dangerous or deep underwater work.

down to the seabed. There, it runs on battery power as it stores information on tape, or transmits it to a research ship. The package may remain on the seabed for weeks while the ship is free to go off and work in another area. When the task is completed, the ship returns and sends down an acoustic signal. Automatic catches then release the package from its heavy base and it pops to the surface on buoyancy floats, where it remains until the ship picks it up.

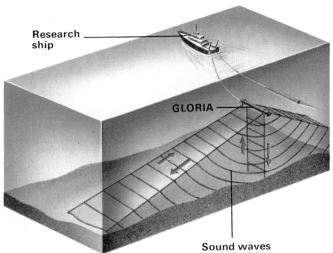

Research ship

GLORIA

Sound waves

▲ **The most advanced side-**scan sonar is the Geological Long Range Inclined Asdic (GLORIA). It scans the seabed up to 18 mi at

either side with pulses of sound, and then converts the echoes into a detailed picture of the seabed landscape and geology.

◄ **The bathysnap camera can** be preset to take flash photos of the seabed every few minutes. Using this camera, new species have been photographed at 4,600 ft in the Atlantic Ocean.

▼ **A bottom dredge is a steel-** framed net that is towed over the seabed on skis. Samples of animal and plant life collect in a small container at the end of the net.

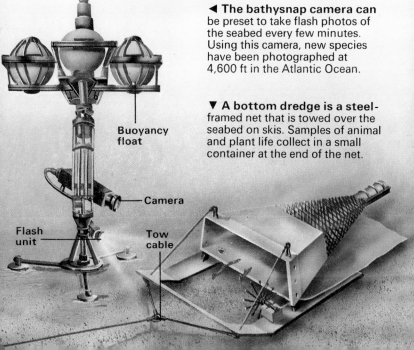

Buoyancy float

Camera

Flash unit

Tow cable

World Oceans and Seas

THE BIGGEST OCEANS AND SEAS

	Area in mi²
Pacific Ocean:	64,186,300
Atlantic Ocean:	33,420,000
Indian Ocean:	28,350,500
Arctic Ocean:	5,105,700
Caribbean Sea:	971,400
Mediterranean Sea:	969,100
Bering Sea:	873,000
Gulf of Mexico:	582,100
Sea of Okhotsk:	537,500
Sea of Japan:	391,100
Hudson Bay:	281,900
East China Sea:	256,600
Black Sea:	196,100
Red Sea:	174,900
North Sea:	164,900
Yellow Sea:	113,500

THE OCEAN DEEPS

	Average depth in feet	Greatest depth in feet
Pacific Ocean:	12,925	35,840
Atlantic Ocean:	11,730	28,232
Indian Ocean:	12,598	23,376
Caribbean Sea:	8,448	24,721
Arctic Ocean:	3,704	17,880
South China Sea:	4,802	15,000
Bering Sea:	4,893	13,500
Mediterranean Sea:	4,926	16,896
Gulf of Mexico:	5,297	17,070

THE LARGEST ISLANDS

Area in mi²

Greenland:	840,000
New Guinea:	306,000
Borneo:	280,100
Madagascar:	226,658
Baffin Island:	195,928
Sumatra:	165,000
Honshu:	87,805
Great Britain:	84,200
Victoria Island:	83,896
Ellesmere Island:	75,767

Ocean Currents

Around the edges of the continents, the shallow coastal waters surge in and out with the tides, and also swirl around in local patterns caused by headlands and bays and the shape of the seabed. Away from the land things are very different. Here, the ocean waters move in great sweeping patterns that are driven by the winds that blow over them.

Near the Equator the main ocean currents travel toward the west, driven by the trade winds. Nearer to the poles, the ocean waters are blown back toward the east by the westerlies (see pages 30–31). The result is that in each of the ocean basins there is a roughly circular movement of water, with warm tropical water flowing away from the Equator in the western parts of the basins and cold water flowing back toward the Equator in the east to complete the loop. These circular patterns are called gyres.

Surface currents

The currents that make up the main ocean gyres move at an average speed of about 6 miles per day, although some of the narrow, warm currents flowing away from the Equator, such as

▶ **This map shows the** world's 38 main surface currents. In equatorial regions the currents are blown toward the west and in polar regions the currents are blown eastward. This creates six roughly circular movements of water called gyres, traveling in a clockwise direction in the Northern Hemisphere and counterclockwise in the Southern Hemisphere.

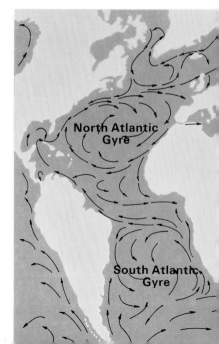

LOST AND FOUND – *TITANIC*

On the night of April 14, 1912, the ocean liner *Titanic* struck an iceberg in the North Atlantic, and sank with the loss of 1,500 lives. This disaster took place south of Newfoundland, where winds blowing first over the warm Gulf Stream and then over the cold Labrador Current create fog banks, and where vast icebergs from Greenland's glaciers drift south into the Atlantic shipping lanes on the Labrador Current.

In 1986 the wreck of the great ship was discovered at a depth of 12,500 ft, and it was photographed by the research submersibles *Alvin* and *Jason*.

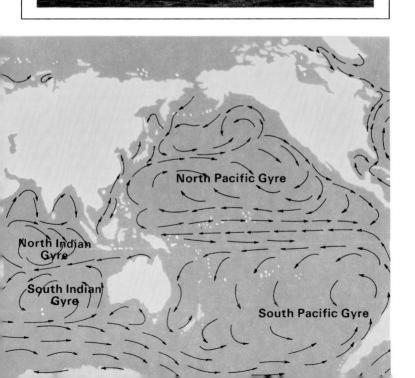

the Gulf Stream and the Kuroshio, may travel 100 miles in a day.

In the Northern Hemisphere the gyres rotate clockwise, whereas in the Southern Hemisphere they rotate counterclockwise. So the big North Atlantic gyre, for example, is made up of the westward-flowing North Equatorial Current; the Gulf Stream, which flows up the east coast of North America; the eastward-flowing North Atlantic Current; and the south-flowing Canaries Current which runs down the coast of northwest Africa back toward the Equator.

Most of the major gyres have smaller current systems around their edges. These systems are fairly constant. Only the currents in the northern part of the Indian Ocean change with the seasons, and this is because of the special wind conditions of the monsoons (see pages 52–53).

Deep ocean currents
The movement of the water deep down in the ocean basins is very different from that on the surface. The effect of the wind does not reach down very far. In fact, the surface gyres are rather like pools of warm water, 1,600–2,600 feet deep, floating on top of the much colder deep ocean water.

Most of this cold bottom water starts off in the polar regions and, because cold water is dense, it sinks and spreads toward the Equator along the deepest parts

of the ocean basins. The main movement is therefore southward from the Arctic Basin and northward from Antarctica and the Southern Ocean. Living conditions are so constant in these deep waters that the sharks that usually inhabit the waters around Greenland have been found at depths of 10,000 feet off the coast of southern California.

Upwellings
Cold ocean waters are much richer in food than the warm surface waters of the Tropics, which is why the icy North Atlantic Ocean holds some of the world's best fishing grounds.

Cold water also creates rich fishing grounds in other parts of the world. Off the west coast of South America, for example,

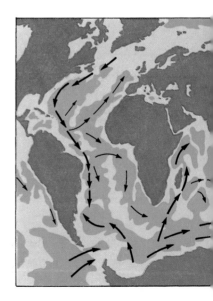

winds blowing offshore push the surface waters away from the coast and this in turn drags up some cold water from down below. The cold water is rich in nutrients and provides food for huge shoals of small fish, such as anchovies. These are caught in vast numbers by the fishing boats of Peru and Chile.

However, the upwelling of cold water is not just important for the fish, it is the basis for a complete food chain (see pages 132–133). The nutrients in the cold water feed microscopic marine plants and animals. These feed the anchovies and other small fish, and these in turn are food for a whole variety of larger fish, and for huge colonies of fish-eating birds such as pelicans and cormorants.

Direction of wind

▲ **Upwellings are common off** the west coasts of continents. Offshore winds push the surface water away from the coast and it is replaced by cold water rising up from lower levels.

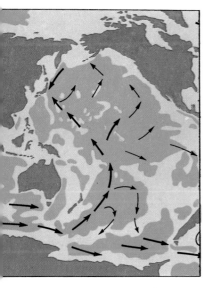

◀ **The cold Arctic waters flow** southward through the deep basins in the Atlantic Ocean. They penetrate far into the Southern Hemisphere until they finally meet the cold bottom waters spreading north from Antarctica. In the Pacific Ocean it is the Antarctic water that travels farthest, reaching almost to Japan before it meets the Arctic bottom waters spreading southward.

Waves

As the wind blows over the surface of the ocean, the friction between the air and the water sets up minute wavelets on the water surface. These wavelets grow steadily bigger and soon develop into small waves whose pointed crests are separated by round, hollow troughs.

At this stage, other forces help to increase the size of the wave. The wind can now press against the upwind side of the crest and push it along. The wind also swirls over the top of the wave and creates an area of low pressure on the downwind side.

Breaking waves

The water particles in a wave move in a circular direction. When a wave enters shallow water there is no longer room for this circular movement and it is squashed into a flat oval. This makes the waves above slow down and pile up. The waves become steeper and unstable and then they break.

On a gently sloping beach the waves spill forward and wash up

▼ **Storm waves crash against** a harbor wall sending plumes of spray high into the air.

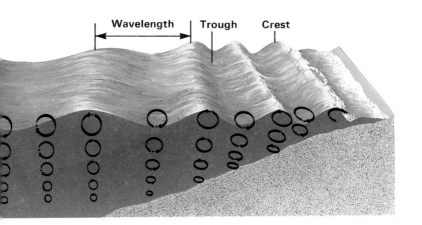

Wavelength **Trough** **Crest**

the beach, breaking gradually. If the slope is steep, however, they are more likely to overturn as plunging breakers.

Water power

The amount of energy locked up in the oceans is enormous. What's more, it is energy that is not harmful to the environment and is endlessly renewable. The one big problem is how to extract it.

In the distant future it may be possible to tap two of the biggest

▲ **The motion of a water** particle inside a wave is almost circular until the wave meets the upward slope of a beach.

ocean energy sources of all: the energy locked up in huge masses of water with different salt concentrations, and the heat energy held in masses with different temperatures.

At the moment, however, engineers are trying to harness the power of waves and tides.

▼ **Rip currents are strong, local** currents. They can be a danger to bathers since they run back out to sea in channels on the seabed.

▼ **When waves strike a beach** at an angle, sand grains are carried along the shore in a zigzag path. This is called longshore drift.

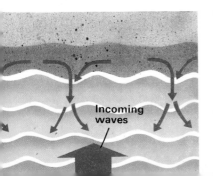

Incoming waves

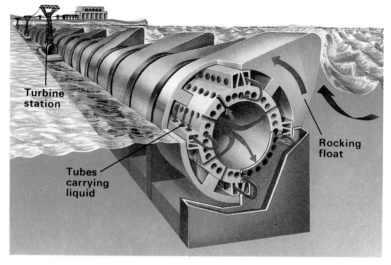

Turbine station

Rocking float

Tubes carrying liquid

▲ **The special shape of the** rocking float absorbs most of the energy of the incoming wave and uses it to drive the pumps inside. These pump a special liquid that spins the turbine blades.

▼ **In this Norwegian air-ram** system the incoming wave pushes air up the tower and through the turbine blades at the top. The retreating wave pulls air back down through the turbine again.

Wave power

Wave-power machines built so far are of two main types. Some, like the "rocking ducks" shown above, use the bobbing motion of the waves to move rocking floats. These floats in turn operate powerful pumps, which force a special fluid through pipes to drive the turbine blades, thus generating electricity. The other main type is called an air-ram system. It uses the powerful surges of incoming waves to drive air through a turbine that is mounted in a tower at the head of a sea cliff. As the waves go up and down, air is forced out of the tower and then drawn back into the tower. Both airflows cause the turbine blades to spin.

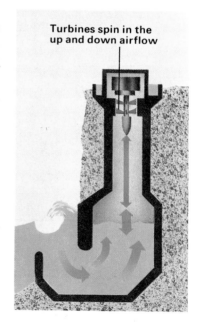

Turbines spin in the up and down airflow

Tides

If you spent the entire day on a beach in Tahiti in the Pacific Ocean, you would notice barely any change at all in the level of the sea. Spend a day in the Bay of Fundy in Nova Scotia, Canada, and you would witness the most spectacular tidal range in the world. Here the difference between the level of the sea at low tide and its level at high tide can be as much as 50 feet.

In most parts of the world the tide surges in and out twice each day as the enormous mass of water in the world's oceans is pulled by the gravitational forces of the Sun and Moon.

On a smooth, water-covered globe this would lead to perfectly regular tides, but the Earth's oceans are separated by irregular-shaped continents, and the ocean basins themselves are broken up by mountain ranges, deeps, island chains, and other obstructions.

The result is a complex pattern of tides that differs slightly from ocean to ocean. Out in mid-ocean the tidal range may be only

▼ **Mont-St-Michel off the** north coast of France is cut off by the tide twice every day.

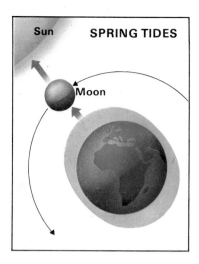

SPRING TIDES

Sun

Moon

▲ **When the Sun and Moon** are in line with the Earth, the effect of two gravitational fields produces the high spring tides at Full Moon and New Moon.

▼ **At the First Quarter and the** Third Quarter the Sun and Moon are pulling at right angles. The pull of gravity is at its weakest and tides are low.

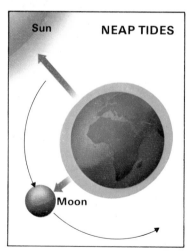

NEAP TIDES

Sun

Moon

three to ten feet; but where the waters wash against the edges of the land, the rise and fall in sea level can be enormously exaggerated by the shape of the continental shelf and by the bays and headlands of the coastline.

Tidal movements

The main cause of the ocean tides is gravity. It is the gravitational pull of the Earth that keeps the Moon fixed in its orbit around the planet. But the Moon also exerts a pull on the Earth, and it is this force that causes the oceans to bulge outward toward the Moon, forming tides.

Because it is very close, the Moon is the main cause of the tides. But the Sun also exerts a gravitational force on the Earth, and depending on the position of the Sun and Moon, this can affect the size of the tide. When the Sun and Moon are in line, at the Full Moon and New Moon, their forces combine and produce the very high tides called spring tides. When the Moon and Sun are pulling at right angles, which happens during the First and Third Quarters of the Moon's cycle, the result is the much lower tides called neap tides.

Lunar gravity explains the bulge of water on the side of the Earth facing the Moon, but it does not explain why we have tides on the far side. These are caused by the way the Earth moves. It may seem as though the Moon travels around the Earth in

▲ ▶ **These pictures** taken in the Bay of Fundy, Canada, at high and low tide show the dramatic tidal range in this narrow inlet.

a circle, at the center of which is the Earth's center. In reality, the Earth and Moon are locked together, and both are moving around a point that is a little way from the Earth's center. The result is that the water on the side farthest from the Moon is thrown outward by the Earth's spin, producing a bulge on that side of the globe also. Each day the two bulges travel once around the Earth, giving us two high tides.

Tidal power

The tidal power station built across the estuary of the River Rance in northern France was the first of its kind in the world. The dam was built right across the river mouth. There are lock gates in it to allow ships in and out.

The dam contains a series of huge turbines housed in tunnels below the waterline. As the tide rises and falls twice each day, sea water surges back and forth through the tunnels, driving the turbine blades. These in turn drive banks of generators which make electricity.

Tidal power will be even more useful when we are able to store energy between tides.

The Ocean Resource

In 1984 the total world catch of marine life was more than 80 million tons – almost four times as much as in 1950. This harvest included fish, mollusks (shellfish, octopus, and squid), crustaceans (crabs and lobsters), and edible seaweed.

Curiously, although almost 9,000 different species of fish are used as food around the world, only 22 species are caught in large quantities. Almost half of all marine fish caught are herrings, cods, jacks, redfishes, and mackerels.

These figures seem to suggest that the oceans contain a vast and endless supply of food. Sadly this is not so. The United Nations Food and Agriculture Organization (FAO) estimates that the absolute maximum sustainable world catch would be about 100 million tons, but long before this figure was reached some of the most popular food species, such as cod and herring, would already be in great danger from

▼ **Inshore fishermen using** cast nets in Sri Lanka.

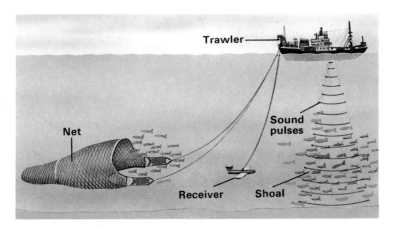

Trawler

Sound
pulses

Net

Receiver   Shoal

▲ **Modern trawlers use echo-**
sounders to locate a shoal of fish.
Sound pulses are directed toward
the seabed. The pulses are echoed
back more quickly when a shoal
comes into range. A monitor
within the net checks that the net
is correctly positioned and this
information is sent to the ship
from a towed receiver.

overfishing. Around the shores
of Europe and North America,
some species are already being
over-exploited.

Fish-catching methods

An enormous number of fish-
catching methods are used
around the world. Some are
very simple and ingenious, while
others require complex and expensive equipment.

In shallow coastal waters and
in lagoons and marshes, fish traps
are common. Some are like mazes
of woven mats that lead the fish
into a central cage. Others are
baited, and are snapped shut by a

springy rod when the bait is
tugged by a fish. In some areas
cover pots or baskets are used.
The fisherman wades slowly
through the marsh and traps the
fish by quickly dropping the pot
over it. The fish is then taken out
through a hole in the top.

Hooks and lines are used in all
parts of the world. Some fishermen use live bait, while others use
lures made of wood or plant fiber
or even spider webs. Spear fishing
and bow-and-arrow fishing are
also common but are more often
used in lakes and rivers.

Nets come in a huge range of
shapes and sizes. Cast nets are
large circular nets with small
weights around the edge. The net
is thrown over a shoal of fish by a
fisherman standing on the prow
of a canoe. One of the most
common methods of fishing from
a beach is seine fishing. A long net
is carried out to sea from the
beach by canoe. It is laid out in a
wide arc and then back to the

111

shore. Then both ends of the net are hauled in – a job that often involves the whole village.

Large-scale deep-sea fishing is carried out from modern boats, with echo sounders to locate the shoals. The big trawl nets used by fishermen in the North Atlantic can yield 80 tons of fish each time the huge bag-shaped net is hauled in. Drift nets are like walls of net hanging from floats. They catch fish by the gills when they swim into the net, and are used to catch herring and mackerel.

Mineral resources
In the late 1950s, scientists studying the Pacific seabed found that large areas were covered in rounded mineral nodules. These consist mainly of manganese but also contain copper, nickel, and cobalt. Various ways of mining these deep-sea mineral deposits have been tried. At the moment it is too expensive, and there are environmental problems to be solved. But in the future, if supplies on land run low, these deposits could be very important.

Seabed sediments on the continental shelves are often rich in minerals that have been washed from the land by erosion. They are much easier to mine than minerals on the deep-sea floor, and are an important source of iron, gold, tin, and platinum, as well as several rarer minerals.

◄ ▼ **Nodules that are** rich in minerals cover large areas of the deep ocean bed. Technology is currently being developed to mine these nodules. The machine on the bottom left works like a deep-sea vacuum cleaner, sucking up the nodules. The machine on the right is a sled that is towed along the seabed to collect nodules and pass them up a tube.

Power from the sea

OTEC (Ocean Thermal Energy Conversion) is the first operational power station to use the 36°F temperature difference between tropical surface water and the cold water far below. The warm water is used to evaporate a special liquid. The resulting vapor is piped through turbines to turn the generators, and the cold water is then used to condense the vapor back to liquid so that it can go around the cycle again.

OTEC systems are still very much in the development stage. The first operational plant was built near Hawaii in 1979 and it ran very successfully. It was a relatively small unit producing just 50 kilowatts of electricity, but it proved that the idea worked: Energy could be generated using only the difference in temperature between warm tropical surface waters and deep waters. Plans are now being made to build a much bigger test unit with a cold water intake pipe 50 feet in diameter and 4,000 feet long.

Systems like this may not be a major source of energy at the moment, but in the future they could prove ideal as a means of supplying power to people on tropical islands.

▶ **The OTEC system uses the** difference in temperature between surface and deep waters to drive a power-generating plant.

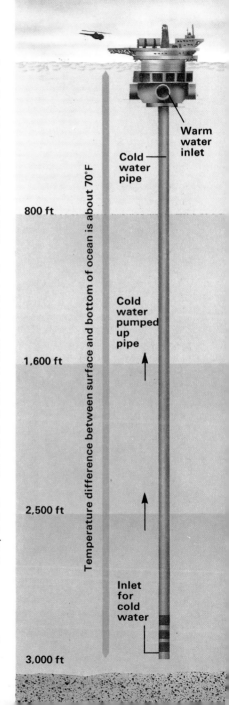

Temperature difference between surface and bottom of ocean is about 70°F

Warm water inlet

Cold water pipe

800 ft

Cold water pumped up pipe

1,600 ft

2,500 ft

Inlet for cold water

3,000 ft

The Living Earth

Animals and plants do not live in separate little worlds of their own. Each one is part of a community – a collection of animal and plant species that live together in the same place. That place is called a habitat. It may be a tropical forest, a barren desert, a marsh, meadow, or the top of a high mountain. Each has a character all of its own. It has a particular climate – hot or cold, wet or dry – and a particular type of vegetation. It will also have an animal population made up of species that are specially suited to that habitat. Some of the animals will be plant-eaters, others will be hunters, and some may be scavengers. Some may even be parasites, living entirely on the bodies of their hosts.

Each species is part of the habitat system, like a single cog in a large machine, and the study of animals and plants and their relationships with their habitat – and each other – makes up the science of ecology. The word ecology is a perfect description of the science. It comes from the Greek word *oikos*, meaning "home," and *logos*, meaning "the study of" or "science of."

▶ **Water, sunlight, and green** vegetation are the basic ingredients of all life on Earth. Without the unique chemical chlorophyll, which gives plants their familiar green color, there would be no food, and so no animal life.

114

Patterns of Climate

The climate of a particular region is the characteristic pattern made up over the year by the region's weather. It is a combination of many factors. The latitude, for example, determines how hot or cold the region will be, and whether the weather changes much from one season to another.

Regions close to the Equator are warm all year-round, and their moist, warm winds bring a steady supply of rain throughout the year. These regions have little seasonal variation in the weather.

Polar regions, surprisingly, have very little rain or snow. Even in a blizzard, most of the snow is being picked up off the ground and blown about by the wind. These regions are cold all year-round, with just a short, milder summer and very long, harsh winters.

In between are the temperate climates. These typically have a warm and fairly dry summer, a short, cold, damp winter, and very marked spring and autumn seasons in between.

▶ **Although no two** places have exactly the same yearly weather pattern, it is possible to group together those places with similar patterns.

These groupings form the main climate types. On either side of the tropical belt lie the monsoon or subtropical zones, and outside these are zones of savanna climate.

Northern hemisphere climates are a mixture of mountain, steppe, and Mediterranean types, produced by the shape of the continents, the mountain ranges, wind systems, and numerous other factors.

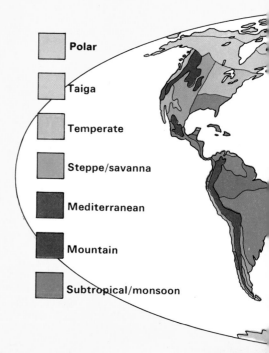

Polar

Taiga

Temperate

Steppe/savanna

Mediterranean

Mountain

Subtropical/monsoon

▲ **Desert landscape in Cadiz Valley, California.** The occasional desert rain allows sparse vegetation to grow.

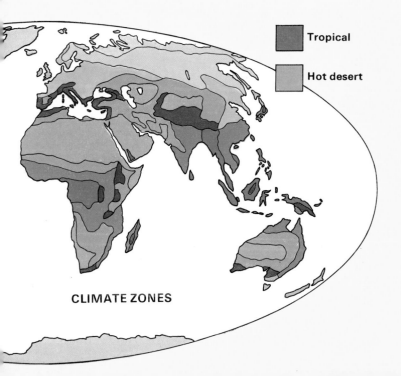

Tropical

Hot desert

CLIMATE ZONES

Another important factor in a region's climate is whether or not the region is close to the sea, and if it is near the sea, on whether the local currents are warm or cold, and which way the wind blows! Britain and northwest Europe, for example, do not suffer extremes of cold because they are permanently washed by the North Atlantic Current which brings warm water across from the Caribbean. The main winds are the westerlies, and these bring in

▲ **Plenty of moisture makes** temperate woodland a rich and varied habitat for wildlife.

warm air from the same direction.

In Namibia and Chile things are very different. These countries also lie on the west side of continents but they have cold currents along their shores, and the main winds are the trade winds, which blow away from the land. This combination produces coastal deserts.

THE LARGEST DESERTS

	Area in mi²
Sahara Desert, Africa:	3,500,000
Gobi Desert, Asia:	500,000
Australian Desert:	467,000
Arabian Desert:	420,000
Kalahari Desert, Africa:	225,000
Chihuahuan Desert, U.S./Mexico:	140,000
Mojave Desert, U.S.:	15,000

TEMPERATURE AND PRECIPITATION PATTERNS
IN THE MAIN CLIMATIC ZONES

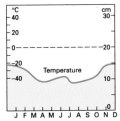

Polar: very long, harsh winters and short, cool summers.

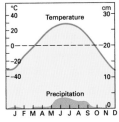

Taiga: long, cold winters separated by short, cool summers.

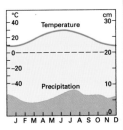

Temperate: four seasons with rainfall throughout year.

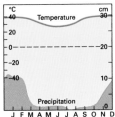

Steppe/savanna: warm winters and summers.

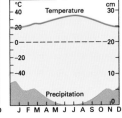

Mediterranean: mild winters and warm summers.

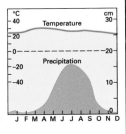

Mountain: variable, according to latitude, height, etc.

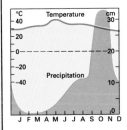

Subtropical/monsoon: hot all year with wet and dry seasons.

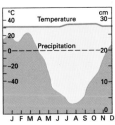

Tropical: hot all year with heavy rain in most months.

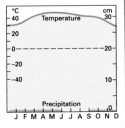

Hot desert: hot year-round with very little rainfall.

40°C = 104°F	0°C = 32°F	−40°C = −40°F	20 cm = 8 in
20°C = 68°F	−20°C = 4°F	30 cm = 12 in	10 cm = 4 in

Vegetation and Soil

The most noticeable thing about the map of vegetation zones on this page is its similarity to the world climate map on pages 116–117. Each region of the world has a natural type of vegetation. The kind of plants that grow in a region, and how much can grow there, is determined first of all by climate.

Plant growth depends on how much sunlight an area gets, how much rainfall it receives, and on how warm or cold it is.

The warmth, bright sunshine, and constant rain of the equatorial regions provide the perfect conditions for plant growth, and it is here that the tropical evergreen rain forests flourish. Temperate regions have good growing conditions for part of the year only, so their natural vegetation types are deciduous woodlands and grasslands.

Where rainfall is low and daytime temperatures are very high, little can grow except the tough scrub plants and cacti typical of desert lands.

▶ **The world has** eight vegetation zones and they are determined by climate. The size and shape of a plant is controlled by the conditions in which it grows. For example, tropical forest trees tower 190 ft or more above the ground as they compete for sunlight. By contrast, mountain and tundra plants are more likely to be about 2 in tall since they need to stay compact and close to the ground to avoid being damaged by the wind. Tropical forest flowers are often huge, whereas those of the mountain plants are usually tiny and tucked away in a dense mass of leaves for protection.

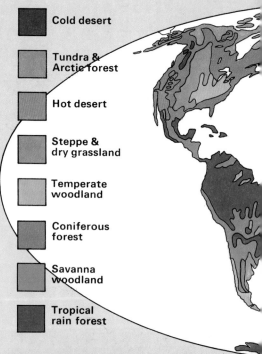

Cold desert

Tundra & Arctic forest

Hot desert

Steppe & dry grassland

Temperate woodland

Coniferous forest

Savanna woodland

Tropical rain forest

▲ **Typical savanna landscape in northeast Namibia is an** open plain of coarse grasses dotted with flat-topped acacia trees.

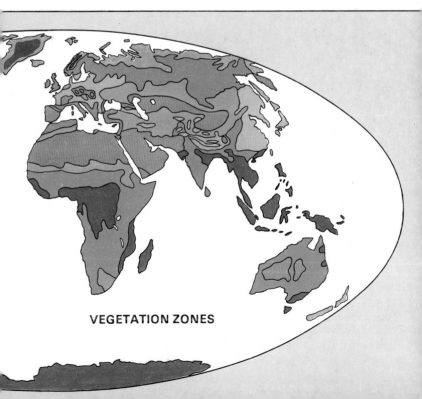

VEGETATION ZONES

Habitat specialists

The kind of plants that grow in any particular area will also be affected by the type of soil, and by other factors such as high winds, flooding, or salt spray. Mountain plants, for example, are usually low and compact for protection from the wind and the drying effect of the Sun. They also have tough, woody roots that can force their way into tiny rock crevices. Coastal marsh plants have had to adapt to other conditions. They must be able to grow in waterlogged ground without their roots and stems rotting, and they must also tolerate saltwater which would kill many other plants.

Soil types

Soil is the layer of loose material lying on top of the solid rock of the Earth's crust. It consists mainly of tiny rock particles and the decomposing remains of plants, called humus. The broken-down rock provides minerals needed for plant growth, and the humus provides additional nutrients and also helps to hold moisture in the soil layer where plant roots can reach it easily.

In dry regions the soil may be only a few inches deep, but in temperate woodlands and grasslands it may be several feet thick. Tropical forest soils are often surprisingly shallow, and if the protective cover of the forests is removed, the soil is soon eroded, or worn away.

▼ **These are six of the most common types of soil.** Soil type depends mostly on climate, but is also affected by the rocks beneath the ground.

▲ **Desert soil lacks moisture.** Because there is very little plant life in the desert the soil is low in humus.

▲ **Tundra soil is often frozen** many feet deep. In the summer the surface layer thaws but it remains wet and badly drained.

▲ Podzols are soils that form under temperate forests. They are usually rich in humus and nutrients, enriched by the autumn leaf-fall.

▲ Latosol is the typical rain forest soil. Plant remains on the forest floor decay steadily, returning nutrients to the soil.

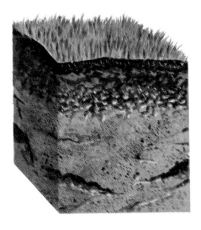

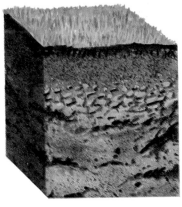

▲ Chernozems are the typical rich, dark soils of the dry, short-grass prairie lands in the western part of the United States.

▲ Prairie soils are deeper, with more humus. They typify the wetter, long-grass prairies in the eastern part of the United States.

123

The Water Cycle

Only 2 percent of the water on Earth is fresh water, and more than 70 percent of that is locked up in the great ice caps of Antarctica and Greenland, the floating ice of the polar seas, and the glaciers of the world's high mountains.

The rest of the world's fresh water is constantly recycled through the atmosphere, rivers and lakes, plants and animals, and rocks of the Earth's crust, until it finally returns to the sea. The diagram below shows roughly what percentage of this circulating water is involved in the various stages of transit or storage at any time.

▼ Of the 84% of water that evaporates from the oceans (1), 77% falls again as rain at sea (2).

Roughly 7% of the evaporated water is carried inland on prevailing winds (3).

Transpiration by plants (4) and evaporation from land and open water (5) account for 16% of the water fed into the atmosphere.

The water carried in from the sea, plus that from the land, add up to the 23% of water held in the atmosphere. This falls as precipitation – rain, hail, or snow (6).

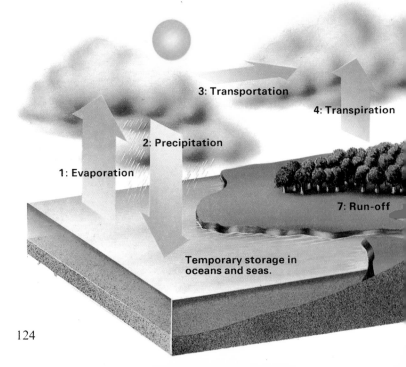

3: Transportation

4: Transpiration

2: Precipitation

1: Evaporation

7: Run-off

Temporary storage in oceans and seas.

Rates of recycling

In the Amazon rain forest a water molecule may fall as part of a raindrop, be taken in by the roots of a plant, be passed out again as vapor through a pore in a leaf, and return to the atmosphere – all in less than a day.

For water molecules frozen into ice, recycling may take a lot longer: up to 10,000 years for a molecule locked in the vast Antarctic ice cap, for example.

In between these two extremes, molecules may spend a few weeks in a river, ten years in a lake, or several thousand years in one of the oceans.

▼ **The diagram below shows** the main processes that keep the Earth's stock of fresh water in constant motion. The more detailed captions on the left show the approximate amount of water involved at each stage in a temperate water cycle.

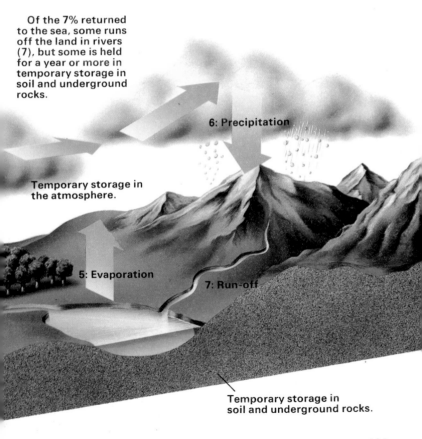

Of the 7% returned to the sea, some runs off the land in rivers (7), but some is held for a year or more in temporary storage in soil and underground rocks.

6: Precipitation

Temporary storage in the atmosphere.

5: Evaporation

7: Run-off

Temporary storage in soil and underground rocks.

World Rivers and Lakes

THE LONGEST RIVERS

	Length in mi
Nile, Africa:	4,160
Amazon, South America:	4,000
Yangtze, Asia:	3,965
Mississippi-Missouri, N.America:	3,710
Ob-Irtysh, Asia:	3,360
Huang He (Yellow River), Asia:	2,905
Amur, Asia:	2,745
Lena, Asia:	2,735
Zaire (Congo), Africa:	2,720
Mackenzie, North America:	2,635
Mekong, Asia:	2,600
Niger, Africa:	2,590
Yenisey, Asia:	2,545
Missouri-Red Rock, North America:	2,540
Paraná, South America:	2,485
Mississippi, North America:	2,340
Murray-Darling, Australia:	2,310
Irtysh, Asia:	2,200
Volga, Europe:	2,195
Madeira, South America:	2,015
Indus, India:	1,800

THE HIGHEST WATERFALLS

	Ft
Angel Falls, Venezuela:	3,212
Mongefossen Falls, Norway:	2,539
Yosemite Falls, California, U.S.:	2,425
Mardalsfossen Falls, Norway:	2,149
Tugela Falls, South Africa:	2,014
Cuquenan Falls, Venezuela:	2,000
Sutherland Falls, New Zealand:	1,904
Ribbon Falls, California, U.S.:	1,612
King George VI Falls, Guyana:	1,600
Gavarnie Falls, France:	1,385
Tyssefallene, Norway:	1,378
Silver Strand Falls, California:	1,170
Wollomombi Falls, Australia:	1,100
Geissbach Falls, Switzerland:	984
Reichenbach Falls, Switzerland:	656

THE LARGEST LAKES AND INLAND SEAS

	Area in mi²
Caspian Sea, USSR/Iran:	143,245
Lake Superior, U.S./Canada:	31,700
Lake Victoria, Kenya/Uganda/Tanzania:	26,830
Aral Sea, USSR:	24,900
Lake Huron, U.S./Canada:	23,000
Lake Michigan, U.S.:	22,300
Lake Tanganyika, Tanzania/Zambia/ Zaire/Burundi:	12,700
Lake Baikal, USSR:	12,160
Great Bear Lake, Canada:	12,095
Lake Nyasa, Malawi/Mozambique/ Tanzania:	11,150
Great Slave Lake, Canada:	11,030
Lake Erie, U.S./Canada:	9,910
Lake Winnipeg, Canada:	9,417
Lake Ontario, U.S./Canada:	7,550
Lake Balkhash, USSR:	7,115
Lake Chad, Nigeria/Niger/Chad:	6,300
Lake Maracaibo, Venezuela:	5,215
Lake Eyre, Australia:	3,600
Lake Rudolf, Africa:	2,475

Nature's Recycling System

In recent years recycling has become an important topic. We now try to avoid wasting paper, glass, and other materials by using them more than once. Yet there is nothing very new in the idea. Nature has been recycling materials for over 4 billion years – and it is just as well that it has, because without an efficient recycling system the Earth's entire surface would long since have been buried hundreds of feet deep in dead vegetation, animal droppings, and decaying bodies.

Bacteria, earthworms, beetles, insect larvae, and molds are not the most popular of living things, but they are certainly among the most important. They are all decomposers – the hidden workers who break down animal and plant materials into their chemical building blocks and return them to the soil, where they can be taken up again by plant roots and used to build new stems, leaves, and seeds.

▼ **These fungi are just the** reproductive parts of the organism. Most of the fungus is inside the tree stump feeding on the dead wood.

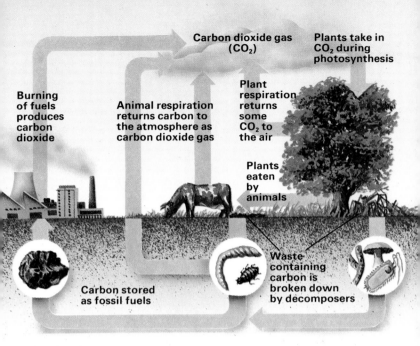

Carbon dioxide gas (CO₂)

Plants take in CO₂ during photosynthesis

Burning of fuels produces carbon dioxide

Animal respiration returns carbon to the atmosphere as carbon dioxide gas

Plant respiration returns some CO₂ to the air

Plants eaten by animals

Carbon stored as fossil fuels

Waste containing carbon is broken down by decomposers

Life's raw materials

All living things on the Earth are made from a limited supply of raw materials, such as the elements carbon, nitrogen, calcium, oxygen, and iron, for example. These are life's chemical building blocks and they must be used over and over again. In the millions of years since life appeared on Earth, the same atoms may have been used in trees, insects, dinosaur bones, and bird feathers, and they will all be used again in the distant future.

As soon as a leaf falls to the ground, or a mouse dies in a bush, the decomposers go to work. Microscopic bacteria play a big part in the process and so do countless molds and fungi. But

▲ **The carbon cycle shown in** the diagram above illustrates how this element is used and reused as it passes from air to plant to animal and finally back to the atmosphere.

other decomposers are large enough to see. Mites, earthworms, millipedes, and other vegetarians chew up the dead leaves and mix them into the soil. Scavengers may eat part of the mouse's body, and beetles may bury parts of it beneath the soil. Flies will lay their eggs on the body so that their grubs will hatch on a mountain of food. Nothing will go to waste. Any nutrients that are not used immediately will be stored in the soil and will be used later by growing plants.

Energy from the Sun

The amount of heat and light energy that the Sun pours onto the Earth each day is equal to the output of millions of power stations. It is this energy that fuels all life on Earth. Without it there would be no plants or animals, no life of any kind.

But animals cannot eat sunlight, and they cannot make the food they need to fuel their bodies, keep them warm, and build new flesh and bone. Only plants can do this, and so all animals obtain their food from plants or by eating other animals that eat plants.

The key to life on Earth lies in

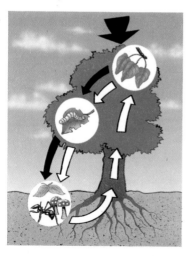

▲ **Nutrients (white arrows)** must be recycled, but the Earth's energy supply (black arrows) is renewed every day by the Sun.

▶ **Photosynthesis takes place** mainly in the large palisade cells that lie just beneath the surface of the leaves. It can, however, take place in any part of a plant that has chlorophyll, including branches, stems, and even roots.

a remarkable substance called chlorophyll – the green pigment that gives most leaves their familiar color. This chemical enables plant cells to trap the energy in sunlight and use it to drive a chemical process called photosynthesis, which means "building with light." The cells take in carbon dioxide from the air, break it down into carbon and oxygen, and combine the carbon with water drawn in by the plant's roots to make sugar. The sugar can then be used as fuel to drive the plant's own processes, or it can be turned into starch and stored for future use. It is these sugar and starch reserves that provide food for the animal kingdom, including ourselves.

At the same time, the oxygen from the carbon dioxide is released into the Earth's atmosphere as a by-product.

In this single chemical process, hidden away inside the leaves and stems of grasses, shrubs, and forest trees, all the world's food is made, and the planet's atmosphere is cleaned and enriched with oxygen.

PHOTOSYNTHESIS

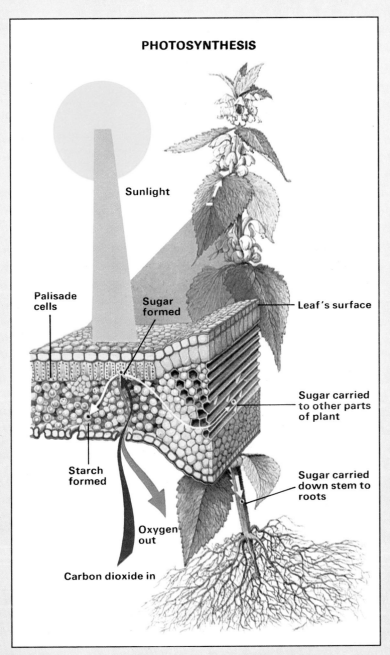

Sunlight

Palisade cells

Sugar formed

Leaf's surface

Sugar carried to other parts of plant

Starch formed

Sugar carried down stem to roots

Oxygen out

Carbon dioxide in

Food Chains and Webs

All animals need a constant supply of food in order to function properly. When the animal is active – especially if it must run or fly fast in pursuit of its food – it may use up an enormous amount of energy in a very short time. And even when an animal is at rest, energy must still be used to keep its body at the right operating temperature and all its systems working.

Many animals are completely herbivorous – that is, they eat only plant food. Obvious examples are sheep, antelope, and elephants. Less obvious are many of the smaller plant-eaters: seed-eating birds and mice; sap-sucking insects such as aphids; and specialists like hummingbirds, which feed only on the nectar of flowers.

Other animals are carnivores, which means flesh-eaters. This group includes hunters as varied as tigers and eagles, dragonflies and bird-eating spiders. It also includes scavengers, which are animals that feed on the scraps left by feeding predators, or on the remains of animals that have died from natural causes. Vultures, jackals, and crabs are scavengers.

▼ **In the savanna habitat the** leopard is one of the top predators: It has no natural enemy other than people. Unlike the other big cats, the leopard will often drag its kill high into the fork of a tree.

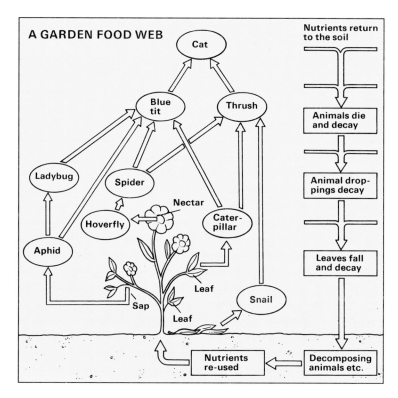

A GARDEN FOOD WEB

Nutrients return to the soil

Animals die and decay

Animal droppings decay

Leaves fall and decay

Decomposing animals etc.

Nutrients re-used

Who eats what?

These groups of animals do not live totally separate lives. They are linked together by their common need for food. A caterpillar feeding on a leaf may suddenly end up as a meal for a bird called a blue tit, which may later be killed by a kestrel or the local cat. Biologists call that a food chain. Energy in the form of food is passed along the chain from plant to plant-eater and then to a first-level hunter and finally to the top hunter (which often has no natural enemy but people).

However, very few animals eat

▲ **The garden food web** works in exactly the same way as that of the jungle or savanna.

only one kind of food. The blue tit eats many different insects and grubs (and some plant food as well). Kestrels also eat a variety of prey. In addition to birds, they eat small mammals such as mice, and frogs and large insects.

Each animal may therefore be part of many different food chains, and as these chains are all interlinked they form what the biologists call a food web. An example is shown above.

Poisoned food chains

In the 1960s, scientists were puzzled by a sudden alarming drop in the numbers of golden eagles, peregrine falcons, and other birds of prey in Europe and North America. For some reason the birds were failing to breed normally. Many of the nests were found to contain broken or badly formed eggs.

Eventually the scientists discovered that the eggs contained high levels of DDT, a chemical used by farmers to control insect pests. Unfortunately, once its job was done, DDT did not break down into harmless substances – it remained in the environment.

Once the DDT entered the food chain it was easily absorbed into the body fat of mammals and birds. Each time a hawk ate an animal contaminated with the chemical, it stored in its body all the DDT that animal had ever eaten. Soon the predators were

▲ Contaminated water
quickly affects whole food chains. If the DDT concentration in the lake (1) is 1 unit, water plants (2) may contain 800 units and plant-eating fish (3) may contain 6,000 units. The next step in the food chain are pike (4) which may absorb 33,000 units, while the top predator, the grebe (5), may contain half a million units.

carrying enormous concentrations of the chemical. Some died as a direct result of the poison, but another effect was to make their eggshells so thin that they broke when the birds tried to sit on them to incubate them. Once DDT was banned, many of these spectacular hunting birds began to recover.

Similar problems arise when certain pesticides get into rivers and streams, and in recent years farmers in Europe and North America in particular have been changing to more "environmentally friendly" pesticides.

A FOOD PYRAMID

▲ **This food pyramid** illustrates how energy is passed from plants to the plant-eaters and then up to the first- and second-level hunters. At each step the energy that an animal uses up to fuel its movements is lost from the chain (shown by the wavy arrows) and only the energy that makes new body tissue is passed onto the animal above.

▶ **The feeding rate** of nestlings is amazing. A pair of adult blue tits, for example, may have to make 500 journeys each in a single day – their beaks full of caterpillars for their hungry young.

Parasites and Partnerships

Apart from a few primitive survivors, most of the plants and animals we see today are very different from the ones that inhabited the Earth millions of years ago. The reason for this is the slow process of change called evolution. In most species the young in each generation get some of their characteristics from one parent and some from the other, and the result of this constant mixing is that some offspring in each generation are slightly different from their parents. In some cases this makes them better equipped than their parents to survive in a changing world, while in others it makes them less well equipped to survive. The ones best suited to living conditions at the time survive and produce young of their own. Less well-equipped species eventually fail and become extinct.

One of the most curious things about evolution is that it has produced a wealth of strange partnerships, some between plants, some between animals, and some involving one of each.

Parasites

A parasite is an animal or plant that gets some or all of its food by stealing it from another animal or plant. Some parasites do relatively little harm to their "host," but many others do great damage or even kill the host.

One of the most familiar plant parasites is mistletoe, usually found growing on apple or oak tree branches. The seed arrives in the droppings of a bird, and soon takes root in the tree bark. Mistletoe is not a total parasite as it has green leaves and can therefore make its own food, but it also sends a mass of fine roots into the tree branch to obtain water and other nutrients.

The most spectacular of all totally parasitic plants must be rafflesia, which grows in the rain forests of Malaysia. It spends almost its entire life underground, attached to the root of a forest vine, but when the time comes for it to reproduce it erupts through the soil with a bud the size of a football. This opens into the world's largest flower – up to 3 feet across – and it smells like rotting meat! Even the smell is part of the plan. It attracts the carrion flies that are the plant's main pollinators.

Among the great "killer" parasites of the plant world are the fungi. Because they have no chlorophyll they are not true plants, so none of them can manufacture their own food. Some are parasites on other plants, especially on trees. The woodland honey fungus may look attractive as it sprouts around the trunk of a tree, but out of sight it has sent a mass of fine rootlike threads into the tree which will eventually kill it.

◄ **A vast flower is the only** part of the rafflesia that is visible. The rest of this parasitic plant consists of threads that are hidden inside the tissues of its host.

▼ **The liver fluke is an internal** parasite that is found in many animals. In the life cycle shown below it has two hosts – a sheep and a snail.

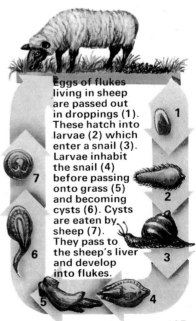

Eggs of flukes living in sheep are passed out in droppings (1). These hatch into larvae (2) which enter a snail (3). Larvae inhabit the snail (4) before passing onto grass (5) and becoming cysts (6). Cysts are eaten by sheep (7). They pass to the sheep's liver and develop into flukes.

137

Animal parasites

Most animals carry parasites on their bodies. Ticks, lice, and mites attach themselves to the skin, while fleas live in the hair and feed on blood sucked from the host's skin. These external lodgers are mostly just a nuisance.

Internal parasites, which live inside the body, usually in the gut or in the blood, are often more dangerous. They include many types of parasitic roundworms and tapeworms, some of which can cause illness in humans.

One of the most dangerous human parasites is the tiny worm-like malaria parasite. It is injected into the body in the saliva of the *Anopheles* mosquito, and once there it multiplies and attacks the red cells in the blood, producing the raging malaria fever.

Hitching a ride

Many partnerships in the plant world do no harm to either of the plants. Trees have strong, woody trunks to hold them up. Most plants have softer stems and do

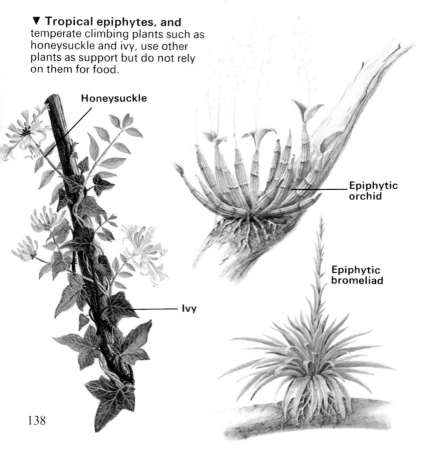

▼ **Tropical epiphytes, and** temperate climbing plants such as honeysuckle and ivy, use other plants as support but do not rely on them for food.

Honeysuckle

Epiphytic orchid

Epiphytic bromeliad

Ivy

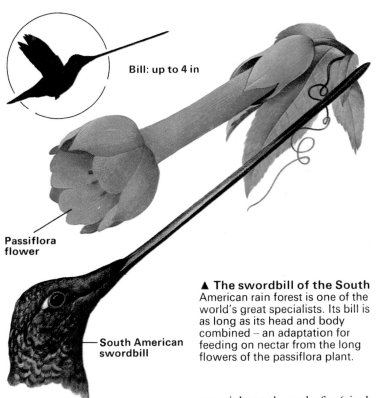

Bill: up to 4 in

Passiflora flower

South American swordbill

▲ **The swordbill of the South** American rain forest is one of the world's great specialists. Its bill is as long as its head and body combined – an adaptation for feeding on nectar from the long flowers of the passiflora plant.

not grow very tall. The climbing plants have evolved a neat trick: They can reach high above the ground without needing strong stems by simply climbing up the nearest tree or bush. Among the most dramatic are the tropical vines and lianas. Some grow to 500 feet or more, looping high into the forest canopy.

Plant-animal partnerships
When Charles Darwin visited Madagascar during his famous around-the-world voyage, he discovered an orchid whose nectar was right at the end of a 6-inch-long tube. Darwin predicted that such a flower could have been pollinated only by a moth with a tongue 6 inches long. At the time people laughed at him, for no such insect had ever been seen. Today we know that Darwin was absolutely right!

Similar pairs of plants and animals are found among the hummingbirds of Central and South America. Birds that feed on nectar from long tubular flowers have long straight bills, while others have deeply curved bills to suit the shape of their own particular food-flowers.

139

Issues of Today

Almost every year the world's newspapers and television screens are dominated at some point or another by a natural disaster of international concern. One year it is flooding in Bangladesh; another year drought and hunger in the dry lands of Africa. Recent years have also produced a succession of major environmental issues, such as acid rain, the dumping of toxic wastes, damage to the ozone layer, and the destruction of the tropical rain forests.

One theme links most of these problems together: people. The world's population is growing at a dizzying pace, and it is growing fastest in areas that are least able to cope. In many developing countries the human population is increasing far faster than food supplies. Although international aid can help to some extent, the terrible scourge of hunger will return again and again until the basic problems are tackled; that is, until population growth can be slowed down and the supply of food made more reliable.

The industrialized nations must also change their ways. Here the problem is not caused by too many people, but by their demands for a standard of living so high that it creates environmental problems on a worldwide scale.

▶ **Almost all of the problems** facing the world today come down to one central issue – the number of people crowding our planet and making ever-greater demands on its living space and resources.

The People Problem

In 1850 the world population was about 1.3 billion. By 1975 it had more than tripled to 3.9 billion and it has now passed the 5 billion mark.

Estimates based on present growth rates show that even though the rate of growth is slowing down, by the year 2025

▼ **The map below shows that** the human population is very unevenly distributed over the globe.

another 3 billion people will have been added to the world population.

Birth rate and death rate

Just how fast the population of a country grows depends on two things – the birth rate and the death rate. These are usually given as percentages. If a country has a birth rate of 5 percent, that means that for every 100 people alive at the start of the year there

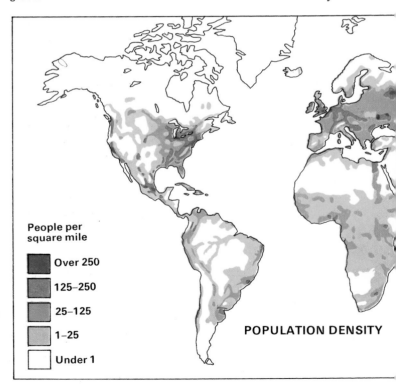

People per square mile

■ Over 250

■ 125–250

■ 25–125

□ 1–25

□ Under 1

POPULATION DENSITY

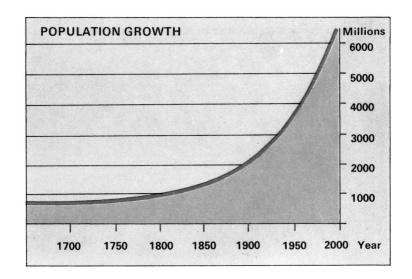

POPULATION GROWTH

Millions: 6000, 5000, 4000, 3000, 2000, 1000

Year: 1700, 1750, 1800, 1850, 1900, 1950, 2000

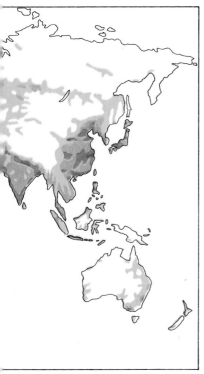

▲ **At the currently estimated** rates of increase, the world's population will exceed 6 billion before the year 2000.

will be 105 by the end of the year. But that is only part of the story. People also die, from old age or illness, and this reduction in population is measured as the death rate.

The real rate of growth is the difference between birth rate and death rate. If the country with the 5 percent birth rate also has a 3 percent death rate, its population will rise by 2 percent each year.

Changes of a few percent may not sound very big, but their effect is enormous. At just over 3 percent, Africa has the highest growth rate in the world. Its effect will be to increase the population of Africa by 695 million people between 1980 and 2010.

143

Population structure

The number of young and old people varies a great deal from country to country. In the developed countries of Europe and America, where the people have plenty of food and very good health care, very few babies and children die, and adults live to a good age. The result is that there are almost the same number of young people as middle-aged people. Because the birth rate is only very slightly greater than the death rate, the population hardly grows at all. (In some European countries the birth rate has dropped so low that the population is actually falling. Both Switzerland and France, for example, are now encouraging people to have children in order to keep their populations stable.)

Developing countries are countries that are economically and socially weaker than developed countries, but are improving themselves. Poor food supplies and lack of health services in developing countries mean that many children there die before they are one year old. Parents therefore tend to have large families. That way they can be reasonably sure that at least some of their children will survive to carry on the family farm or business, and also to look after them in their old age. Unlike farmers in the richer countries, farmers in developing countries cannot afford to employ labor, so the land must be worked by the family alone. There are also none of the welfare services for the old and

◄ **A crowded street** in Rawalpindi, Pakistan. As the population of the developing countries increases, more and more people drift to the cities.

▲ An Indian birth-control poster contrasts a
small, well-fed family with a large and hungry family.

THE WORLD'S LARGEST CITIES

	Population (1990)
Tokyo-Yokohama, Japan:	26,952,000
Mexico City, Mexico:	20,207,000
São Paulo, Brazil:	18,052,000
Seoul, South Korea:	16,268,000
New York, U.S.:	14,622,000
Osaka-Kobe-Kyoto, Japan:	13,826,000
Bombay, India:	11,777,000
Calcutta, India:	11,663,000
Buenos Aires, Argentina:	11,518,000
Rio de Janeiro, Brazil:	11,428,000
Moscow, USSR:	10,367,000
Los Angeles, U.S.:	10,060,000
Manila, Philippines:	9,880,000
Cairo, Egypt:	9,851,000
Djakarta, Indonesia:	9,588,000
Tehran, Iran:	9,354,000
London, UK:	9,170,000
Paris, France:	8,709,000
Delhi, India:	8,475,000
Karachi, Pakistan:	7,711,000
Lagos, Nigeria:	7,602,000

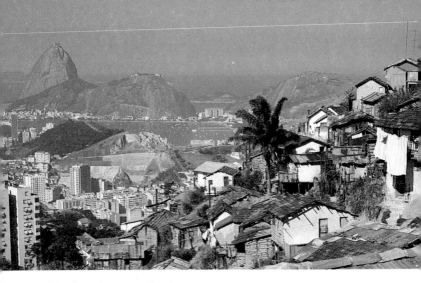

sick that there are in developed countries so the family does this job too.

Because of these factors, the developing countries tend to have large numbers of young people and relatively few old people in their populations.

▲ **Shantytowns cover the** hillsides round Rio de Janeiro, Brazil.

What is to be done?

Some countries have already taken steps to reduce their growth rates. China, with a population of more than 1.1 billion people, has taken the most drastic action. There, it is now against the law for couples to have more than one child. In India the government is using persuasion rather than force. Rewards have been introduced to encourage people to use birth-control methods to limit the size of their families.

However, changing people's behavior and traditions can be a difficult and complex task. In some Roman Catholic countries,

for example, this task is further complicated since the church is opposed to the use of birth control.

Many countries also face great practical problems. They may have a huge, scattered, rural population that is difficult to reach. In addition, most of the people are likely to be un-educated. So, before it is possible to start teaching birth control, the government must send trained people around the villages explaining to the people *why* it is important for them to have fewer children.

The growth of cities

The problem of population growth is clear to see in many of the big cities of the world's developing countries. People in poor rural areas flock to the cities in search of jobs and a better standard of living. All too often there are no jobs for them when they get there, and they are forced to live in dirty shantytowns clustered around the edges of the city. Bogotá, for example, capital of Colombia, had about 35,000 inhabitants in 1940. Today it has more than 3 million – over half of them living in makeshift shelters on the city's outskirts.

The drift to the cities is not new. It happened all over Europe during the Industrial Revolution in the nineteenth century. The big difference now is that it is taking place on a much larger scale, and it is combined with extremely high birth rates in the cities. In Kenya, for example, the country's population growth is just over 4 percent, but in major cities such as Mombasa and Nairobi it is a massive 7 percent.

Urbanization – the movement of people into the cities from rural areas – brings many problems in addition to the misery and hunger of people forced to live in overcrowded slums. Poverty and hunger make shantytowns a breeding place for disease and crime, and sooner or later the misery turns to anger and political unrest aimed at the wealthier citizens, the city authorities, and finally the government.

▼ **By the year 2000 there will** be 12 more cities with over 10 million inhabitants each. This will bring the total number of "mega cities" to 25, and 21 of them will be in the developing world.

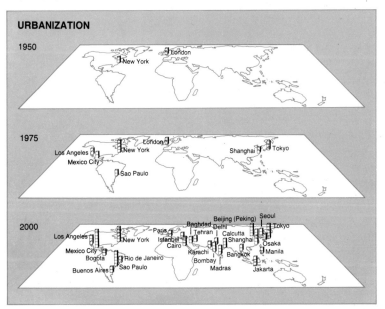

URBANIZATION

1950

1975

2000

Raw Materials and Energy

The constant growth in the standard of living of people in the industrialized countries of Europe, North America, Japan, and Australasia means that these countries are constantly demanding more energy to heat their homes, and more fuel and raw materials to keep their industries supplied. At the same time, many of the world's developing countries want to improve their own standard of living. They can see the cars, televisions, and other goods that the industrial nations have, and see no reason why they too should not enjoy some of these luxuries.

Unfortunately, sources of energy and raw materials are not evenly spread around the world. The United States and the Soviet Union are both rich in minerals, but they require such a huge volume of raw materials that both have to import extra supplies. Canada, Australia, South Africa, and Brazil also contain great mineral wealth, and because they produce more than they need, these countries are able to export large quantities of these valuable commodities – mainly to the United States, Europe, and Japan.

▼ **One of the world's biggest** open-pit copper mines – the Bingham Mine in Utah, U.S.

▲ **An oil field in the Middle East** with flare stacks burning off the unwanted gas.

Many of the countries of Southeast Asia, Africa, and South America, on the other hand, cannot reap the full benefit of their mineral resources. They have few large manufacturing industries of their own and so are unable to make much use of their store of minerals. They are forced to sell them to other countries. It is an economic trap for the developing countries, because in addition to receiving poor prices for the minerals they export, they also lose out on the thousands of jobs that manufacturing industries could provide.

Some countries are now taking steps to halt this unfair drain on their resources. For example, in 1989 Thailand banned the export of logs, and is now building up her own furniture-making industry. The country thus receives more money for the wood it produces and also gains valuable employment.

Sources of power

A hundred years ago coal was the main source of industrial energy, and today it is still widely used in power stations. However, burning coal produces a great deal of air pollution, and converting power stations to meet new anti-pollution laws can be expensive.

Now, oil and gas are industry's main fuels. They are cleaner, but there is a price to pay. Like other resources, the world's oil and gas supplies are not all conveniently located in the countries that need them most. The U.S. is the world's biggest user of energy, and although it has some oil reserves of its own it also has to import a large amount. The USSR is more fortunate. It contains some of the world's largest reserves and so does not have to depend on outside supplies.

149

The oil-producing countries of the Middle East contain 56 percent of the world's known oil reserves. This gives them considerable influence over the industrial countries because the price those countries have to pay for oil affects the cost of producing their manufactured goods.

Nuclear power is another source of energy. France provides about a quarter of its total energy in this way. However, some people are concerned about the safety of nuclear power, especially after the serious accident in the power station in Chernobyl in the USSR, in 1986.

Some countries have the option of hydroelectric power – that is, electricity produced by water power. Canada produces a surplus of hydroelectricity which it exports to the U.S.

▲ **This woman in Zaire may** have had to walk for half a day to collect this bundle of firewood or to buy it from a trader.

FIREWOOD SUPPLY

The firewood crisis

One startling fact is often overlooked when talking about energy, and that is that nearly half the world's population depends entirely on one fuel – wood. In some of the poorest African countries this single fuel provides up to 90 percent of all the energy used to heat homes, cook food, and power industries.

In 1981 the United Nations Food and Agriculture Organization (FAO) estimated that 2 billion people depended on firewood – and that over 1.1 billion were either suffering from serious fuel shortages already, or were surviving only by cutting down trees faster than they could be replaced. The FAO's estimate for the year 2000 is even more alarming: Unless the current situation can be improved, by then there will be 2.4 billion people dependent on firewood.

The firewood crisis can be solved only with the help of the richer nations. Most rural people in developing countries have no electricity or gas in their homes. The only real solution is to provide long-term supplies of firewood by establishing large plantations of fast-growing trees. This is one of the main aims of the United Nations Food and Agriculture Organization.

▼ **The firewood crisis is now** affecting hundreds of millions of people across Latin America, Africa, and southern Asia.

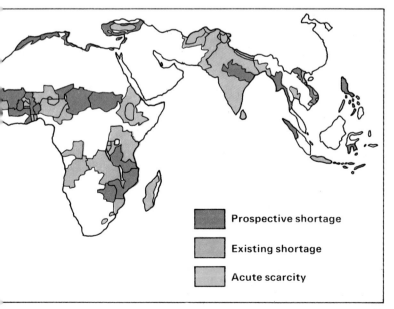

Prospective shortage

Existing shortage

Acute scarcity

Alternative Energy

There are two main problems with coal, wood, oil, and gas as sources of energy. One is that they are nonrenewable resources, which means that once they are burned to produce heat energy they are finished, and we must immediately dig or drill for more. The other is that using them has certain drawbacks. Burning these fossil fuels produces smoke and gases that are harmful – both at ground level where they create smog and damage plant life, and high in the atmosphere where they add to the "greenhouse effect" (see page 168).

Much cleaner and safer ways of producing energy do exist. Just as the waves and tides offer a clean, renewable form of energy, so too do the Sun and the wind. The only problem here is that so far wind power and solar power have only been produced in relatively small amounts. They are unable, for example, to replace coal and oil as the power source for huge cities or big industrial regions.

Energy from the wind

Wind-powered generators can provide cheap electrical power to farms and small communities, and their use is growing year by year. They are efficient, and once they have been installed costs for maintaining them are low.

◄ Facing directly into the winds blowing in over the Pacific Ocean, this California wind farm is ideally placed to take advantage of this clean, renewable source of energy.

▲ **The mirror units at this** solar energy farm in the U.S. automatically tilt as they follow the path of the Sun each day.

In California, hundreds of large wind generators have been set up on "wind farms" using the constant winds that blow in from the Pacific Ocean. By the end of the century wind farms could be producing almost 10 percent of California's energy.

Wind farms have also been built in Denmark, India, and the Netherlands, and more are planned in Britain, Spain, Mexico, and other countries. Because they are relatively simple to maintain, wind-powered generators could also be an important source of energy on islands, where fossil fuels are rarely found.

Energy from the Sun

The first solar-powered cells were developed in the 1950s but they were very expensive to make. However, new materials and advances in microchip technology have changed all that. Experts now believe that within just a few years it will be possible to produce electricity from solar panels for about the same cost as a small oil-powered generator.

When this breakthrough is reached, the Sun could be used to provide electricity for millions of people in countries where fossil fuels are in short supply and traditional firewood supplies are vanishing. Small solar-powered pumps are already providing water supplies for villages in parts of Africa.

153

The Loss of the Forests

The evergreen rain forests that encircle the equatorial regions are by far the richest and most varied of the world's natural habitats. They are also the least explored, the least understood, and perhaps the most important for the future health of the planet.

One of the great ecological disasters of the twentieth century is that the rain forests and the tropical deciduous forests are being lost before we even know what they contain. Every year 47,000 square miles of tropical forest are cut down. The land area of New York State is 47,224 square miles.

▼ **Layer upon layer of thick** vegetation provides a great range of habitats for mammals, birds, reptiles, and insects in this Venezuelan rain forest.

Earth's richest habitat

Tropical forests contain more animals and plants per square foot of ground than any other habitat on Earth. They cover only about 6 percent of the Earth's land surface, yet they may contain up to 90 percent of all the animal and plant species on Earth – perhaps as many as 30 million species.

The most varied woodland in temperate regions may contain 20 different kinds of trees, while the same area of rain forest in the Amazon Basin might contain 200 tree species and thousands of other plants.

Just how rich the rain forests are can be judged from a study of one small reserve in Costa Rica. There, in an area of only 3 square miles, biologists counted 1,125

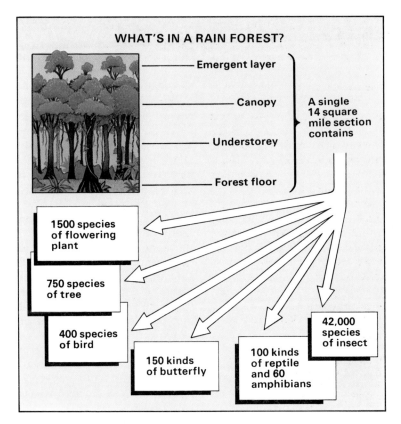

WHAT'S IN A RAIN FOREST?

Emergent layer

Canopy

Understorey

Forest floor

A single 14 square mile section contains

1500 species of flowering plant

750 species of tree

400 species of bird

150 kinds of butterfly

100 kinds of reptile and 60 amphibians

42,000 species of insect

species – one and half times as many as there are in the whole of California, which has an area of over 155,000 square miles.

The rain forests are a vital part of the Earth's life-support system. This huge mass of vegetation takes in enormous quantities of carbon dioxide each day and in return pumps fresh oxygen into the planet's atmosphere. Burning the forests not only robs the atmosphere of this cleansing system, but the fires themselves pour large amounts of carbon dioxide

▲ **The variety of life in a** tropical forest is richer than in any other natural habitat on Earth.

into the air, adding to the "greenhouse effect."

The last great resource
So far, biologists have studied only a tiny proportion of the tropical forests' plant life, yet the forests probably contain hundreds of valuable medicines and food plants. An important anti-malaria drug, quinine, comes

155

from the cinchona tree which grows in the Andes. One of the most effective drugs used for treating the disease leukemia comes from a tropical bush from Madagascar. In fact, almost a quarter of the drugs now in use are made from tropical forest plants or are copies of chemical compounds found in tropical forest plants.

A similar story of riches can be told about food plants. Most of the food eaten in the developed countries comes from about 20 main food plants. By contrast, some forest tribes make use of several hundred different plants in their diet. This great variety of edible plants is a valuable resource.

Who is killing the forest?

Several different groups of people are damaging forests in tropical regions – and each for a different reason. In some cases the people are forced into doing things that damage the forest, and we should not be too quick to blame them. If it comes to a choice between cutting down trees to make room for crops, or of going without food, the trees will obviously be cut down. However, in other cases the cause of forest destruction is simple greed – a desire to make profits quickly, instead of using the forest resource slowly and carefully so that it lasts indefinitely.

Slash-and-burn agriculture

In many forest areas a major cause of damage is slash-and-burn agriculture. A farmer and his family cut down and burn a patch of forest, and plant their crops. The ash left from the fire is like fertilizer and helps the crops to grow. But the rain forest soil is very thin, and after two years it

◄ **The rosy** periwinkle, a tropical shrub native to Madagascar, is just one of many tropical forest plants that have yielded valuable medicines.

is exhausted. The farmer must move on and clear another plot.

When the number of farmers moving around was small, the cleared patches were well spaced out and abandoned plots had plenty of time to recover. Now there are too many people farming this way, and large areas of forest are just a patchwork of old farm plots, half-regrown, with hardly any original forest left between them. The only way of stopping this kind of destruction is to teach the farmers a new way of life based on agricultural methods that make use of the forest without harming it.

Settlers

Some countries that are rich in tropical rain forest have cleared

▲ **Slash-and-burn cultivation** is practiced in forests all over the world. The farmer cuts down the trees and then burns them so that the ash fertilizes the ground. Unfortunately, it is an inefficient and wasteful way of using the forest, since the soil can only sustain crops for a very short time.

large areas of forest and brought in thousands of settlers from outside. In many cases these settlers are poor people from overcrowded cities or overpopulated rural areas. They are often moved for political reasons – to prevent unrest in the big cities, or simply to establish claims to territory by pushing large numbers of people into areas that might be claimed by a neighboring country.

157

Most of these people have no idea what the forest is like, let alone how to make a living in it. The result is often the destruction of large areas of forest for no benefit at all, because within a few years the land is exhausted and the people move out, often suffering from malaria and other diseases. (A hidden danger of clearing the forest is that disease-carrying insects that normally live in the trees come down to ground level.)

At the same time, the habitat has been damaged forever, and very often the native forest tribes have been wiped out or forced away from their traditional lands.

▲ **New roads and settlements** have brought thousands of settlers into the Amazon.

The impact of roads

Of all the world's rain forests none has suffered more in recent years than the Amazon. Vast areas of this forest were cleared in order to build the Trans-Amazon Highway and other roads.

The idea was to "open up" the great untouched rain forest, allowing in the logging companies and many thousands of new settlers. A 12-mile-wide strip of land along the major roads was divided into small farm plots for the settlers. But the scheme was a disaster. The soil is so poor that most of the farms failed and the settlers headed back to the cities. The same mistakes were made in parts of Southeast Asia, where tens of thousands of settlers were moved into forest areas – only to leave again after a few years of misery.

The cattle barons

The only people who gained from settlement policies in the Amazon were the powerful landowners and cattle ranchers who bought up large areas of forest (or pushed the settlers out by force) and cleared them for cattle-raising.

They were helped by generous grants from the government – and that was where most of the profit lay because even the cattle farms were failures. The rough grass that grows where the forest was burned makes poor grazing, and the skinny cattle produced no prime beef – just low-grade meat that was only fit for export for making hamburgers.

A new deal

Now, government planners in many tropical forest countries realize that cutting down the forest is a terrible waste of their natural resources. It is far better to cut just some of the valuable timber trees, leaving others to provide seed for new trees, and to gather the nuts, fruits, resins, and other natural products that the forest renews year after year. At the same time, new farming

THE REAL COST OF A HAMBURGER...

The choices people make when shopping in the U.S. can be felt thousands of miles away. The true cost of a burger made from beef raised in the Amazon is half a ton of rain forest lost for every quarter-pounder!

methods are being developed that enable small farmers to grow a mixture of crops alongside natural forest plants without damaging the soil or losing the forest.

Sustainability

The slash-and-burn farmer and the cattle rancher have one thing in common. They both move into the forest, use it for a while, and then move on, leaving the forest damaged forever.

International organizations such as the FAO are trying to encourage sustainable use of the forest – that is, methods of using the timber, and the plant and animal food of the forest without causing damage. That way, the forest resource will last far into the future.

Soil Erosion

If a hundred people were asked to list the ten most important natural resources on Earth, how many would include soil? Probably none of them, yet in many ways it should be on top of the list. Without this layer of powdered rock and organic material there would be very little plant life, and without plants there would be very few animals. Much of the Earth's surface would be like a desert, and humans would still be living in small bands gathering roots and berries and sometimes catching small animals. The vast areas of cropland and pasture that now feed 5 billion people simply could not exist.

Upsetting the balance

When a habitat is left alone it is a stable, well-balanced system. The soil provides the plants with food and with a firm roothold, and in return the plants protect the soil. Their roots bind the soil and prevent it from being washed or blown away, and the shelter of the leaves protects it from heavy rain.

▼ **The highlands of**
Madagascar have suffered severe soil erosion since the protective forest cover was removed.

Soil is easily damaged when this balance is upset. Over large parts of the Himalayas, for example, people have cut down nearly all the trees and bushes that once covered the hillsides. The wood has been used as fuel and the leaves as fodder, or feed, for yaks and buffaloes. The result is an ecological disaster because the torrential rains of the monsoons have swept the thin layer of soil downhill leaving the hillsides bare. The trees and bushes cannot grow again on the bare rock, and to make matters worse, the wasted soil is carried by the rivers into the lowlands where it silts up dams and drainage systems and blocks the turbines of hydro-electric power stations.

▲ **Removal of the forest in** highland regions affects land and people hundreds of miles away. Without the forest the land is quickly eroded by the rains. The soil is swept into rivers where it blocks irrigation systems and dams and causes flooding in the lowlands.

Lessons can be learned from ages past. Some rice terraces in Southeast Asia have been in use for centuries, feeding the people and protecting the hillsides. Modern terracing is one way of rescuing badly eroded hillsides. Fast-growing trees and bushes are planted on the terraces to provide firewood and animal fodder, and food crops for people are planted among them.

161

Holding back the desert

From newspaper and television pictures of starving people in Ethiopia and Sudan it would be easy to think that this region has always been desert. But this is not true. Northeast Africa may have rather low rainfall, but the natural vegetation over very large areas up to a hundred or so years ago was a mixture of dry grassland and woodland.

The damage here has been done by the enormous growth of both the human population and the herds of cattle and goats that are part of the traditional way of life. The animals eat all the vegetation and what is left is burned as fuel. The soil is trampled by hooves, dried by the Sun, and very soon becomes dust where few plants can grow. The desert quickly takes over.

Scientists are working on new

▲ These terraces in Nepal are protecting the fragile hill slopes from damage by erosion and also providing food for the local people and fodder for their livestock.

ways of using plants to hold back the desert. Tough desert grasses with masses of roots are used to anchor sand dunes and stop them from swamping oases and farms. Fast-growing trees are planted to provide fuel and animal feed.

What is more, these plants help make the soil usable again for agriculture. Their roots anchor the soil, and many of them have the added ability of putting nitrogen back into the soil, which will help other plants to grow. Also, the protective shade of the trees allows other crops to be grown in between them. One of the trees that fulfills all these functions is the Leucaena.

THE ALL-PURPOSE SUPERTREE

Leucaena has been one of the success stories of tropical agriculture in areas where forest cover has been lost and where soil has been damaged. It grows very quickly in a wide range of habitats, and it has a multitude of uses.

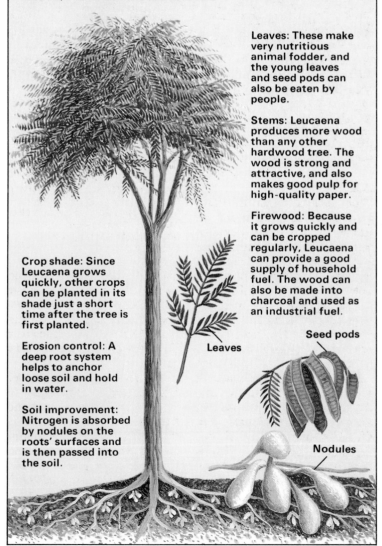

Leaves: These make very nutritious animal fodder, and the young leaves and seed pods can also be eaten by people.

Stems: Leucaena produces more wood than any other hardwood tree. The wood is strong and attractive, and also makes good pulp for high-quality paper.

Firewood: Because it grows quickly and can be cropped regularly, Leucaena can provide a good supply of household fuel. The wood can also be made into charcoal and used as an industrial fuel.

Crop shade: Since Leucaena grows quickly, other crops can be planted in its shade just a short time after the tree is first planted.

Erosion control: A deep root system helps to anchor loose soil and hold in water.

Soil improvement: Nitrogen is absorbed by nodules on the roots' surfaces and is then passed into the soil.

Leaves

Seed pods

Nodules

Air Pollution

When people return to towns and cities after a few days in the country or at the seaside, they nearly always remark on how clean the air smelled on vacation and how dirty the air smells in cities. What most people notice first is the smell of vehicle-exhaust fumes since they are a problem in all towns. In large industrial cities, however, car exhaust is just one of many air pollutants.

▼ **Chemical smog over Los** Angeles shows itself as a dark haze. The smog irritates people's eyes and throats, and causes many deaths from chest ailments.

The invisible hazard

The four main groups of air-polluting chemicals are carbon monoxide and carbon dioxide, oxides of nitrogen, oxides of sulfur, and tiny particles of solid matter that are carried into the air mainly in smoke.

In 1980, the total output of these four pollutants by the industrialized countries was estimated to be 164 million tons (mt) of carbon monoxide, 40 mt of nitrogen oxides, 60 mt of sulfur oxides, and 17 mt of smoke and fine dust particles.

These pollutants are a danger

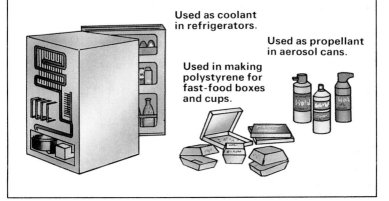

THE OZONE-KILLING GASES

CFCs (chlorofluorocarbons) are chemical compounds. They are normally stable, but high in the atmosphere they are broken down by the Sun's ultraviolet light. These reactions are damaging the Earth's protective ozone layer.

Used as coolant in refrigerators.

Used as propellant in aerosol cans.

Used in making polystyrene for fast-food boxes and cups.

to health and a threat to the environment (see pages 166–169), and so most countries are making great efforts to reduce the amount they produce. Many cities in the U.S. and Europe are either "smokeless" or have zones where making smoke is prohibited. Industries such as steelmaking, oil refining, chemical processing, and power generation in particular, have had to clean up their acts.

Curbing the car
In cities, one of the worst polluters is the car. Or rather, millions of cars pumping out smoke, fumes, and, in many countries, the deadly chemical lead, which is added to gas to improve the performance of the car engine.

The U.S. phased out leaded gas in 1986. The 12 members of the European Community are also changing to unleaded fuel, although much more slowly. But in the huge cities of the developing world the amount of lead in city air is still increasing, and it is a major health hazard. In some large cities, even in Europe, studies have shown that the lead in the air is still well above the safety limit.

In small towns and in open country, car exhaust quickly becomes diluted or blown away, but in cities, especially those built in hollows, the polluted air can become trapped. Even worse, in a city such as Los Angeles, special atmospheric conditions can hold the layer of polluted air over the city for days, and the action of strong sunlight on the air produces a dark haze of chemical smog.

The hole in the ozone layer

Between 6 and 30 miles above the Earth, molecules of oxygen are altered to form ozone. This gas is a health threat at ground level, but high in the atmosphere it performs an essential function by absorbing dangerous ultraviolet radiation from the Sun.

Between 1975 and 1985, British scientists working in Antarctica discovered that the ozone layer over the south polar region had become very thin, and the "hole" – as big as the U.S. – was getting bigger. One of the main causes was a group of gases called chlorofluorocarbons, or CFCs. These are commonly used in aerosol cans, refrigerators, and fast-food packaging.

At an international conference in 1985, 28 nations agreed to reduce their use of CFCs and to

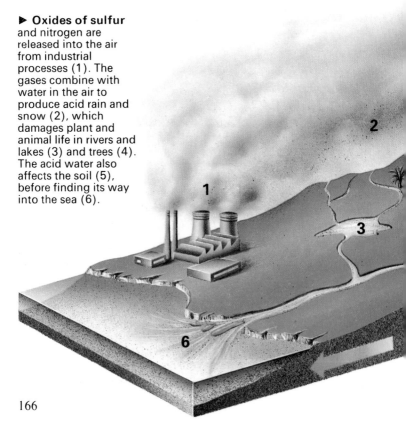

▶ **Oxides of sulfur** and nitrogen are released into the air from industrial processes (1). The gases combine with water in the air to produce acid rain and snow (2), which damages plant and animal life in rivers and lakes (3) and trees (4). The acid water also affects the soil (5), before finding its way into the sea (6).

give high priority to protection of the ozone layer.

Acid rain

In the 1960s, biologists in Sweden discovered very high concentrations of the gas sulfur in the air. They also found that many of the country's lakes were so acid that water plants, fish, and other aquatic animals were dying. Soon after this, scientists in Germany found that large areas of forest were showing signs of damage. These problems were all caused by "acid rain" which is

▲ **Fraser firs damaged by acid** rain falling on Mount Mitchell in North Carolina, U.S.

now known to exist right across Europe, much of the U.S. and Canada, and in parts of many of the world's developing countries.

Acid rain is a simple term for a whole series of chemical processes. First of all, sulfur dioxide and oxides of nitrogen are pumped into the air from factory chimneys. Some of this acidic material combines with moisture in the atmosphere and produces acid rain and snow, which can fall to Earth many hundreds of miles away from the source of the pollution.

In addition to killing plants and damaging buildings, this acid rain and snow can also react with minerals in the soil, robbing the local vegetation of nutrients.

167

The Greenhouse Effect

The greenhouse effect is not new – it has been operating for millions of years. What is new is that human activities have upset the system – and the greenhouse is getting warmer.

It works like this: The Sun's rays pass through the atmosphere and warm up the Earth's surface. The Earth then radiates some of this solar energy back into Space. Most of it passes straight through the atmosphere – but not all. Some gases, such as carbon dioxide, methane, and water vapor, stop this heat energy from escaping.

▼ **The greenhouse effect is** trapping heat energy and raising the Earth's temperature.

These gases act like the glass of a greenhouse – letting the heat in but not letting it all out again.

In the past this system was nicely balanced. The amount of heat kept in by the natural "greenhouse gases" in the atmosphere was just enough to keep the Earth at a steady overall temperature. However, in the last hundred years the balance has been upset. Starting with the Industrial Revolution in the middle of the nineteenth century, more and more carbon dioxide has been added to the atmosphere from factory chimneys and power stations. In the last 20 years the increase has accelerated alarmingly.

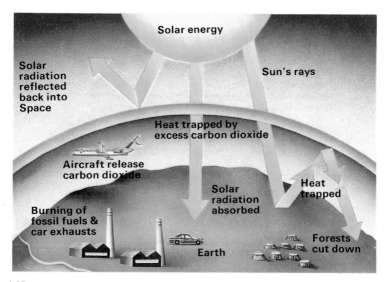

Solar energy

Solar radiation reflected back into Space

Sun's rays

Heat trapped by excess carbon dioxide

Aircraft release carbon dioxide

Solar radiation absorbed

Heat trapped

Burning of fossil fuels & car exhausts

Earth

Forests cut down

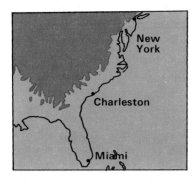

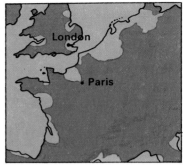

From studying the amount of carbon dioxide in the ice of old glaciers, we know that in 1850 the amount of carbon dioxide in the atmosphere was about 270 parts per million (ppm). Today the proportion has risen to 330 ppm. Over 64 percent of the extra carbon dioxide comes from industry; over 35 percent from the burning of forests. The result is that for the last hundred years the Earth's temperature has been steadily rising.

▲ **Scientists have tried to** estimate the rise in sea level that would result if part of the polar ice melted. These maps show the flooding that could happen in North America and Europe.

Scientists are not yet able to be certain what the longterm effect of this warming will be, but many fear that some of the polar ice fields may melt, raising the sea level and flooding huge areas of low-lying coastal land. Others predict changes in climate that could have a disastrous effect on crop production all over the world. Most, however, agree that global warming is very dangerous, and that all nations should take steps to reduce the amount of greenhouse gases they release into the atmosphere.

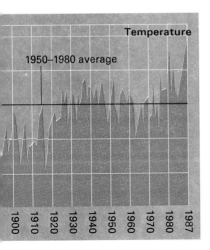

Temperature

1950–1980 average

1900 1910 1920 1930 1940 1950 1960 1970 1980 1987

◀ **For the past 100 years the** average temperature of the Earth has been rising. The temperature graph gradually steepens, then accelerates over the last 20 years. Scientists use the world average from 1950–1980 as a baseline.

The Waste Problem

When pollution of the land, sea, or air is the result of a single major environmental disaster, it makes headlines all around the world. Accidents such as the explosion at the nuclear power station in Chernobyl, USSR, or the massive crude oil spill off the coast of Alaska when the *Exxon Valdez* oil tanker ran aground, are major news stories that run for weeks. But accidents like these account for only a small proportion of world pollution.

Most of the damage is done by an endless series of smaller industrial spills, leaks, and accidents; by inefficient pollution-control systems in factories; and by people dumping waste materials illegally.

Modern societies produce such a huge amount of waste material, from industrial waste to household rubbish, that simply getting rid of it is now a major industry.

Hazardous waste

Chemical and petrochemical industries around the world produce a huge variety of waste products that are either poisonous (toxic), explosive, or otherwise dangerous. Many of them are produced during the manufacture of such everyday things as plastics, paints, adhesives, cosmetics, and fertilizers.

Most of this waste ends up being dumped in holes in the ground. For some waste this is quite safe, but problems arise when many different chemicals are dumped together because some of them react to produce yet more new substances. One big problem with this kind of dumping is that chemicals can seep through the ground and contaminate water supplies.

Many chemical waste products can only be disposed of safely by burning them in very high temperature incinerators. These, however, are expensive to build,

▲ A recent example of waste dumping occurred in 1988 when toxic chemicals from Italy were dumped in Nigeria.

and there are simply not enough of them to cope with the volume of waste that needs burning. This shortage of proper facilities has even led to cases of highly toxic waste being illegally dumped in some developing countries.

▲ **The Rio Tinto river in Spain** is stained with copper from nearby industrial sites and is now almost devoid of any life.

Radioactive waste

One of the most difficult wastes to deal with is radioactive material. This is material that is chemically unstable, which makes it extremely dangerous. It is particularly difficult to dispose of since it can remain radioactive for years.

Nuclear power stations run on fuel rods made of the radioactive metal, uranium. When the rods come to the end of their useful life they are sent for reprocessing. The rods are crushed and soaked in acid, and the remaining uranium is removed and used to make new rods. The highly radioactive liquid waste is then stored in huge tanks that are buried very deep underground, as the waste is too dangerous to release into the environment.

Some radioactive waste is much less hazardous and will gradually lose its radioactivity. This includes such items as clothing and tools used by workers in the power stations, or in hospitals where low-level

171

radioactive materials are used. This waste is put in steel and concrete drums and then either buried on land or dumped at sea.

▲ Greenpeace, one of the leading environmental pressure groups, here in action trying to stop waste dumping at sea.

The problem of sewage

A city of one million people produces over 500,000 tons of sewage every year. In most developed countries this sewage is processed to make it safe before it is flushed into the sea or rivers. But even today a large amount is dumped into the sea partly treated or even untreated.

The problem is even greater in the developing countries because processing facilities are often poor, and much of the partly treated sewage runs into rivers that are also used to provide water supplies, not just to the fields, but often to whole villages.

Household waste

Disposing of household waste is a major task for any city. Each day a mountain of paper, glass, cans, food scraps, and other domestic waste is produced.

Most domestic rubbish is buried, but suitable sites near cities are harder and harder to find. Also, people are now becoming more concerned about wasting the Earth's resources by burying rubbish that could be reused or recycled. The result is that waste is now sorted. Rubbish that cannot be reused is still buried, or burned in incinerators, but more and more of the glass, metal, and paper is now recycled.

RECYCLING WASTE

Recycling waste such as glass, paper, and tin saves on the Earth's resources that are used to make these things. In addition, recycling saves on fuel since less heat is needed to recycle things than to make them from the beginning.

Glass

Paper

Vegetable matter

Tin and aluminum

◀▲ **Glass bottles and jars are** collected in bottle banks and then melted down to make new glass. Paper and cardboard can be pulped and made into paper again. The tin and aluminum in metal cans is often melted down to make new cans, instead of mining more metal. Vegetable matter can be left in a compost heap where it will rot back into the earth.

The Threat to Wildlife

Loss of Habitat

All over the world, people are altering natural habitats for their own use. Forests are cut down to provide timber, or so that the land can be used for growing crops or for raising cattle. Coastal marshes and other wetlands are drained to make way for farms, cities, and holiday resorts. Woodlands and meadows disappear beneath new concrete highways, and remote islands are stripped down to bare rock so that valuable minerals can be mined.

Some of these activities are necessary. People do need space to build houses, and room to grow their food, but very often wild habitats are used without any thought for what happens to the local wildlife – and innocent people often suffer as well. When the forests of Sri Lanka were cut down for their valuable timber, for example, so much soil was washed into the coastal lagoons that local fisheries were ruined. And it is not just the forests and animals of distant lands that are threatened. Over much of mainland Europe native toads, frogs, and snakes have been wiped out over large areas because their natural habitats have disappeared under farmland, roads, or housing developments.

◄ **The coarse grasses eaten by** these cattle in the Amazon Basin will shelter and feed only a few birds and insects. By contrast, the forest that used to stand here was home to hundreds of species.

▲ **Even in the late 1980s ivory** poachers killed more than 80,000 African elephants each year. Some deaths are a total waste: here, the killers fled without even taking the tusks.

The killer trade

Illegal hunting and collecting is one of the biggest threats to wildlife in many parts of the world. Elephants have been killed in the thousands by poachers who want their tusks for the ivory trade. Rhinoceroses have been almost wiped out in parts of Africa and Asia, again because of their valuable horns. Many of the world's most beautiful cats, including the clouded leopard, snow leopard, and tiger, were hunted to the edge of extinction for their fur, and even now are all listed as rare and protected species.

Even today, illegal catching and smuggling of rare birds is a multi-million-dollar worldwide business. Some of South America's rarest parrots and macaws are now almost extinct because collectors will pay tens of thousands of dollars for a single live bird. Hundreds of birds die during attempts to capture them. And of the birds that are caught, up to three-quarters die either during transportation or on arrival at their destination.

Tourists beware!

Street markets are a tourist attraction in many countries, and most have stalls selling souvenirs made from shells, horns, teeth, feathers, coral, and other materials. They seem innocent enough, but visitors should be careful about what they buy. Each time a piece of coral is sold, another piece must be hacked off the reef to take its place on the stall; and for each feather fan that is bought, several more birds will be killed to keep up the supply.

How rare is rare?

We know much more about some groups of animals than we do about others. People have been studying mammals and birds for a long time, and we probably now

▲ **Scientists estimate that** more than 20 million birds are traded worldwide every year.

▼ **The flightless kagu is one** species that will be lost forever if the rain forests are destroyed.

know most of the world's species. Even so, many of them live in tropical forests and are hardly ever seen. Some, in fact, have not been seen again since the day they were first discovered, and in some cases that was 50 years ago!

It is therefore difficult to know exactly when a rare species finally becomes extinct. The last definite sighting in the wild of a *thylacine*, or "Tasmanian wolf," was in the 1930s, and most people thought it was now extinct. However, in 1984 the Tasmanian Wildlife Service released a report that one had been seen in 1982, so this rarest of mammals may survive even now.

At least 150 bird species have become extinct in the last 400 years, but the threat today is far greater than ever before. Now, more than 1,000 species are officially listed as being in danger – and that is one in ten of all the bird species known.

The deadly chain effect

Even though we know far less about the world's insects and plants than we do about birds and mammals, we do have a fairly good idea of the total number of species there are in each of the main animal and plant groups. This has enabled biologists to work out the true cost of destroying the world's natural habitats. It now seems certain that for every mammal species that disappears into extinction, the world also loses as many as 200 other animal species (some of which we may never even have heard of) and about 70 plant species.

Animals and plants are now disappearing faster than ever before in the Earth's history, and only people have the power to stop the destruction. If we fail, the balance of nature could be permanently upset and the world will lose forever a priceless resource.

▶ **The hidden losses** of animal and plant life quickly mount up. For each mammal species that becomes extinct we lose two bird species, up to six fish, about 70 plants, and as many as 180 species of insect.

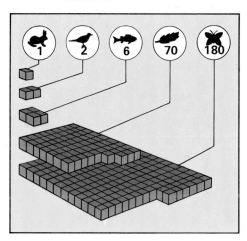

Conservation in Action

Animals and their habitats can only be protected if we really understand how they function, so the first requirement is for detailed scientific research.

In many countries there is a shortage of trained scientists, so locally trained biologists often work with visiting scientists from the wealthier nations.

Training and education

Nations also need effective nature conservation organizations. These are not cheap, but they are essential. They need trained people and modern equipment, and must be supported and paid for by the government.

In Kenya, rangers look after the large national parks and the wildlife within them. However, for many years, ivory poachers in Kenya could do as they pleased. They had powerful radios, and better guns and faster vehicles than the rangers. Some even used planes to track the elephants. Now things are different. Kenya's rangers are fully equipped, and more than a match for the poachers.

Kenya has also led the way in Africa by setting up Wildlife Clubs in all the schools. Kenya now has a generation of young people who are interested in their wildlife and habitats – and also know a great deal about them, and how best to protect them.

Changing public opinion

People often think there is nothing much they can do to change what is going on in the world, but public opinion is a surprisingly powerful weapon. Not long ago, expensive coats made from ocelot, wild mink, or Arctic fox fur were worn very proudly by rich and famous people. Today, in most of Europe and America at least, such coats are rarely seen. One of the main causes of the change in public opinion was a massive advertising campaign against killing animals simply to satisfy part of the fashion business.

What you can do for nature

You do not have to live in Africa to help conserve the elephant, or in South America to want to protect the rain forest. People everywhere can help the conservation movement by becoming involved in conservation groups, by giving support to wildlife appeals, and by making an effort to learn more about environmental issues.

◀ **American biologist Donald Perry** was one of the first to use a high-level spider web of climbing ropes as a means of studying the rain forest canopy at really close quarters.

▼ **An effective kind of reserve** has a core area where animals and plants are totally protected. Around this are buffer zones where research and some other human activities are permitted.

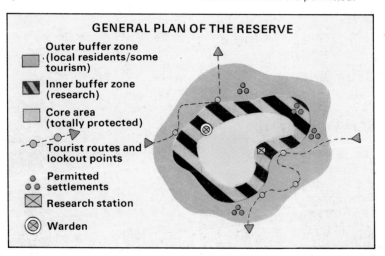

GENERAL PLAN OF THE RESERVE

- Outer buffer zone (local residents/some tourism)
- Inner buffer zone (research)
- Core area (totally protected)
- Tourist routes and lookout points
- Permitted settlements
- Research station
- Warden

Glossary

Acid rain
Rainwater that has been made acidic by dissolving the sulfur and nitrogen oxides given off by burning coal, oil, and gas.

Acoustic
Anything to do with sound.

Anticyclone
A high-pressure weather system that usually brings settled, dry weather.

Aurora
A display of colored light in the sky in the north or south polar regions. It is caused by particles of solar radiation hitting molecules of gas high up in the Earth's atmosphere.

Barometer
An instrument for measuring atmospheric (air) pressure.

Carnivore
An animal that feeds mainly or entirely on the flesh of other animals. Cats, seals, eagles, and snakes are all carnivores.

Chlorophyll
A remarkable green chemical that is found in the leaves and stems of plants. It has the special ability of using the Sun's energy to drive the food-making process of photosynthesis.

Cirrus
Very high cloud, usually seen as a thin sheet or as wisps with hooked ends. It forms at altitudes of 20,000 feet or more, where it is so cold that the cloud consists of ice crystals rather than water droplets.

Conservation
The protection and wise use of the Earth's plants, animals, water, minerals, and other natural resources for the benefit of everyone, now and in the distant future.

Continental shelf
The submerged edge of the continent. Just offshore, the seabed slopes downward very gently across the continental shelf, but at about 650 feet there is a sudden change. Here, at the edge of the shelf, the seabed drops away steeply to the deep-sea plains below.

Core
The innermost region of the Earth. It consists of two parts: a solid inner core of iron and nickel, and a liquid outer core surrounding it.

Crust
The Earth's outer layer: 4 mi thick under the oceans and 25 mi thick under the land.

Cumulus

Dense, white clouds that are usually flat-bottomed but with domed or cauliflower-shaped tops. Small cumulus clouds are common in fine sunny weather, but they may also grow into the towering cumulonimbus clouds that bring thunderstorms.

Cyclone

A low-pressure weather system that usually brings wind, rain, and generally unsettled weather conditions. Cyclones are also called depressions.

Decomposers

A general term for animals and plants that help to break down the remains of other creatures so that their chemical building blocks can be used again. The most important decomposers are bacteria and fungi.

Deposition

The dumping, or laying down in layers, of mud, silt, sand, and other debris that has been eroded from the Earth's surface. See Erosion.

Depression

See Cyclone.

Drift net

A large fishing net that hangs like a curtain in the water. It has floats along the top edge and weights along the bottom. Fish swim into the net and are caught in it by their gills.

Ecology

The study of living organisms and the way they relate to each other and to their environment.

Epicenter

The point on the Earth's surface directly over the focus of an earthquake (the point at which the rock layers actually break and move).

Erosion

The process of wearing away the Earth's surface. Erosion is mainly caused by water, wind, and ice.

Evaporate

To change from a liquid to a vapor. A puddle dries out on a warm day because all the water evaporates into the air.

▼ **Gathering fodder for the** buffalo can take an entire day for this Himalayan woman. And as the hillside vegetation is removed, the rains slowly erode the soil, leaving bare rock.

Evolution

The slow process of change that takes place in animals and plants over very great periods of time. In each generation the offspring get some of their characteristics from one parent and some from the other. This constant mixing produces young with a range of characteristics, and some are better equipped than others to survive in an ever-changing world.

Fodder

Plant food that is collected or grown specially for feeding animals.

Folding

The bending and buckling of the rocks of the Earth's crust due to earth movements. The Appalachians of the eastern U.S. are folded mountains.

Fossil

The remains of an animal or plant, or the trace of a footprint or raindrop, that has been preserved in a layer of sedimentary rock. Studying fossils from all over the world has enabled scientists to see how animals and plants have evolved over the past 3 billion years.

Front

The boundary zone between two masses of air with different properties. Most depressions form where cold, dry polar air meets warmer, more moist air.

Geophone

A special microphone used to pick up the echoes of shock waves that are created by explosions set off in the ground during geological surveys.

Greenwich

The place in London from which all lines of longitude are measured. The 0° line runs through Greenwich and the 180° line runs down the middle of the Pacific Ocean. (All the international time zones are also measured from Greenwich).

Habitat

The place in which a plant or animal lives, such as woodland, grassland, river, or sea.

Herbivore

An animal that feeds entirely on plant food. Antelope, cows, rabbits, sloths, snails, and tortoises are all herbivores.

Igneous rocks

A general term for all rocks that have formed from molten magma. Intrusive igneous rocks are those that have cooled slowly, deep underground; extrusive rocks are those that poured out onto the surface from volcanoes and so cooled much more quickly.

Industrialized countries

Countries whose economies depend on manufacturing goods for their own use and for trade.

Isobars
Lines drawn on a weather map joining places with the same atmospheric pressure.

Latitude
A measure of the distance of a place north or south of the Equator.

Lines of latitude encircle the Earth parallel to the Equator, which is the 0° line. The lines are in degrees since they are measured as an angle from the Earth's center.

Light-year
A unit of distance used for measuring the vast distances in Space. One light-year is the distance traveled by a ray of light in a year – roughly 6 trillion miles.

Lithosphere
The rocky outer shell of the Earth, made up of the crust and the solid uppermost part of the mantle.

Longitude
A measure of the distance of a place east or west of the 0° line which runs through Greenwich in London.

Like the lines of latitude, longitude lines are measured in degrees. However, unlike latitude lines, they are not parallel: they start from one pole, widen out to the Equator, then narrow again until they meet at the opposite pole – just like the segments of an orange.

Lunar
Anything to do with the Moon.

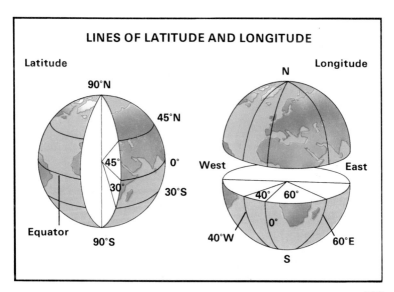

LINES OF LATITUDE AND LONGITUDE

Magma
The molten material that makes up most of the Earth's mantle and is the source of all the different igneous rocks.

Mare (plural maria)
The word means "sea" and was used to name the large, dark areas on the Moon. We now know these areas are huge lava flows, not seas, but the original name is still used.

Marine
Anything to do with the sea.

Metamorphic rocks
The name used for a large family of rocks that started life as igneous or sedimentary rocks but were later changed by heat and pressure.

Meteor
One of numerous small bodies traveling through Space. They may enter the Earth's atmosphere as fireballs or shooting stars.

Meteorologist
A scientist who specializes in the study of weather.

Paleontologist
A geologist who specializes in the study of fossils and the history of life on Earth.

Parasite
An animal or plant that lives entirely at the expense of another.

Plant parasites include many kinds of fungi and molds, and the mistletoe that grows on oak and apple trees. Animal parasites include tapeworms and fleas.

Photosynthesis
The process by which plants manufacture food. Chlorophyll in the plant's cells enables the leaf to combine water (drawn up by the roots) and carbon dioxide (taken in through pores in the leaf) to make sugar and starch.

Precipitation
A general name that covers rain, sleet, hail, snow, mist, and dew – all the ways in which water reaches the Earth's surface.

Predator
An animal that lives by hunting other animals. Lions, hawks, and snakes are all predators.

Renewable
Something that can be replenished or replaced when it has been used. Wind and wave power are renewable energy resources. Coal, oil, and gas are nonrenewable. Once burned they are gone for good.

Rift valley
A steep-sided, flat-bottomed valley formed by large geological faults. The block of the Earth's crust that forms the valley floor has dropped down relative to the blocks at either side, which often form block mountains.

Satellite
A small heavenly body that orbits around a larger one. Earth has one satellite – the Moon. Since the late 1950s hundreds of artificial satellites have been placed in orbit around the Earth. Some of these are for research use, many are for communication systems, and some are for military purposes.

Scavenger
An animal that lives by feeding off the leftovers of other animals. Scavengers are very important since they keep the environment clean and healthy by recycling dead animal matter.

Sedimentary rocks
Rocks that have formed from sand, silt, mud, and other sediments, which have been laid down at the bottom of ancient seas and lakes.

Solar
Anything to do with the Sun.

Strata
The horizontal layers, or beds, that are characteristic of most sedimentary rocks.

Subduction zone
A region of the Earth's surface where one crustal plate is being forced down beneath the edge of another. These zones are areas of intense geological activity; earthquakes and volcanic eruptions are common.

Sustainable
Something that can be kept going far into the future. The tropical rain forests could provide a sustainable source of food, timber, new food plants, and new medicines, but only if they are protected and used wisely. The target in many of the world's poorer countries is sustainable agriculture – that is, farming the land without using up all of its resources.

Transpiration
The process by which plants give off moisture through the tiny pores in their leaves.

Trawl net
A large, baglike fishing net that is towed behind a fishing boat.

Tsunami
The Japanese name for the huge devastating waves that are caused by submarine earthquakes or volcanic eruptions. (They are also called "tidal waves" but in fact have nothing to do with tides.)

Urbanization
The rapid growth of towns and cities, and the movement of people into those cities from the surrounding countryside.

Waning
Getting smaller. The word is often used to describe the Moon as it fades from the Full Moon to the New Moon. The opposite is waxing – getting bigger.

Index

Page numbers in *italic* type refer to illustrations. Page numbers in **bold** type refer to glossary entries.

A

acid rain   *166*, 167, **180**
aerosol   *165*
Africa   73, 74, 78, *142*,
    143, 149, 151, 153,
    162, 179
African plate   *74*
agriculture   144, 156,
    158–*163*, 174
air current   *49*
air mass   29, 36, 40, **182**
air pollution   *164*–167
air pressure   30, *32–33*,
    34, *34*, *35*, 52, 53, **180**
air temperature   29–30
Alps   61
altocumulus cloud   *38*,
    42, 43
altostratus cloud   38,
    38–39, *42*, 43
aluminum   *59*
Amazon Basin   125, 155,
    158–159, *158*
Amazon River   126
ammonite   *87*
Amur River   126
Andes   *76*
Angel Falls   127
animals   129, 159:
    conservation   178, *179*
    extinct   174, *175*, 177
    evolution   88–89, *89*,
        136
    food   130, 132–135
    habitat   13–14, 114,
        154, *155*
    parasites   138
    partnership   138–139
Annapurna, Mt.   71
Antarctica   73, 74, *74*,
    124, 125, 166
Antarctic Circle   *19*
Antarctic Ocean
    102–103

anticline   *78*
anticline trap   *84*
anticyclone   *34*, **180**
aphid   132, 133, *133*
Apollo spacecraft   14–15
Arabian Desert   118
Aral Sea   127
Arctic Ocean   *102–103*
Arctic Circle   19, *19*, 23
ash   156, *157*
Asia   53, 74, 149, 159
asteroid belt   8
Atacama Desert   44
Atlantic Ocean   72, 92,
    93, 102, *102–103*, **182**
atmosphere   24–30, *26*,
    27, *124–125*, **180**:
    global warming
        168–169
    pollution   164,
        166–167
atoll   76, 77
aurora   *27*, 28, **180**
Australia   73, 74, 148
Australian Desert   118
autumn   22, *22*, 23
axis   18, 19

B

bacteria   **181**
Baffin Island   99
Baikal, Lake   127
Balkhash, Lake   127
barometer   **180**
basalt   58, *64*
Bay of Fundy   107, *109*
bird   132, 133, 134, *154*,
    155, 177
bird smuggling   175
birth control   146
birthrate   142–3, 144,
    147
blue tit   133, *133*, 135

Borneo   *99*
Bogotá   147, *147*
Brazil   148

C

calcium   *59*
calendar   18
California   153, 154
Canada   148, 150
carbon   129, *129*, 130
carbon cycle   *129*
carbon dioxide   24, *129*,
    130, *131*, 155, 164,
    168, *168*, 169, **184**
carbon monoxide   164
carnivore   132, **180**
Carrara marble   *69*
Caspian Sea   127
cat   *133*, 175, **180**
cave   *66*, 67
Chad, Lake   127
chalk   67
Challenger, HMS   90
charcoal   *163*
chemical waste   170–171
Chernobyl   150, 170
Chihuahuan Desert   118
Chile   103, 118
China   146
chinook wind   33
chlorofluorocarbons
    (CFCs)   *165*, 166–167
chlorophyll   130, **180**,
    184
circulation cells   30, 31
cirrocumulus cloud   *42*
cirrostratus cloud   38, *39*,
    42
cirrus cloud   38, *39*,
    42–43, *42*, 45, **180**
city   *145*, 146–147, 164,
    165, 172
climate   116–119,
    116–119, 169

cloud 6, 35, 38–39, *38–39*, 40, 40–43, 44–45, 50, **180, 181**
coal 83, 149, 152
cold front *36–37*, 37, *37*, *38*, 39, *54*, 55
Columbia module 14, 15
Cocos plate 94, *94*
conglomerates 65
coniferous forest *120–121*
conservation 178–179, **180**
continent 58, 72–75, *73*, *74*, **180**
continental shelf 92, **180**
continental slope 92
copper 83
coral reef *76*, 77, 176
core 58, *58*, *59*, *82*, **180**
Coriolis force 31, 32, *32*
cosmic rays *27*
Costa Rica 154
crust 24, 56, 58, *58*, *59*, 72, 73, *74–75*, 75, 78, *78*, *82*, 89, **180, 182**, **183, 184**
crustal rocks *74–75*, 75, 77
crystals 62, 63, 79
Cuquenan Falls 127
cumulonimbus cloud 38, 39, 43, *43*, 46, 49, **181**
cumulus cloud *38*, 39, 42, *43*, **181**
current:
 ocean 33, 53, 100, 102, *102–103*
 surface 100, *100–101*, 102
cyclone *35*, **181**

D

dark spots 10
Darwin, Charles 139
date line 20, *21*
DDT 134
death rate 142–143
decomposers **181**
decomposition 128–129, *129*, *133*

Denmark 153
deposition **181**
depression 36–37, *36–37*, *39*, **181, 182**
desert 29, 44, *116–117*, *118*, *119*, 120–121, 162
developing countries 140, 144, 148, 151, 171, 172
dew 40, 41
Dhaulagiri, Mt. 71
dike *63*
Djakarta 145
drift net 112, **181**
dumping waste 170–172

E

earth movements 66, 68, 70, *70*, *79*
earthquake 56, 75, *80*, 80–81, *81*, *82*, 84, **181**, **185**
echo-sounding 95, *111*, 112
eclipse 16–17, *16–17*
ecology 114, 154, **181**
electricity 47–48, 113, 151, 152–153
elephant 175, *175*, 178
Ellesmere Island 99
energy:
 alternative 152–153
 fuel 151
 heat *168*
 industrial 148, 149
 plant *135*
 solar 130, *130*, *131*
 wind power 152–153
environment 24, 134, 140, 152, 164–165, *165*
epicenter **181**
Equator *19*, 29, 30, 31, 100, 116, **183**
equatorial zone 49, 154
equinox 22, *22*
Erie, Lake 127
erosion 61, 65, 122, 160–162, *163*, **181**
Eurasian plate *74*
Europe *169*

evaporation **181**
Everest, Mt. 71
evolution 88–89, *88*, 136, **182**
exosphere *26*
export 148, 149, 150
Exxon Valdez 170
extrusive rocks 63, *64*
Eyre, Lake 127

F

FAO *see* United Nations Food and Agricultural Organization
farming 144, 156–157, 158–159, 160, 161, 162, 174
fault *74*, 78–79, *80*, *93*, **184**
feldspar 63
fish catching 102, 110–112, *111*
flower *120*, *155*
fodder **181, 182**
fog 41, *54*, *101*
fold 68, *75*, 78–79, *78–79*
folding **182**
food 140, 144, 156
food chain 103, 132, 133:
 poisoned 134, *134*
food pyramid *135*
food web 133, *133*
forest *120*, 122, 154–159
forest burning 155, 156–157, 159, *168*, 169
forest destruction 154, 156–159, 161, 167, 174
fossil 66, *72*, 86, *86–87*, 88–89, **182, 184**
fossil fuels 83, *129*, 152, 153, *168*
France 150
frog 174
frontal zone 29, 38, *39*, **182**
fuels 83, *129*, 148–149, 151, *163*
fungus 137, **181**

G

galaxy 11
gas 24, 26, 29, 40, 149, 151, 152, 165
gas, natural 83, 84, *84–85*, 89
Gasherbrum, Mt. 71
Gavarnie Falls 127
Geissbach Falls 127
geological survey **182**
geophone **182**
geophysical prospecting 83–85
Gibbous moon *13*
glacier 61, 70, *70*, 169
global warming 168–169
Glossopteris 72
gneiss 69
Gobi Desert 118
Gondwanaland 73, *73*
Gosainthan, Mt. 71
granite 63, *64*
grassland 120, *120*, 122
gravity 13, 24, 26, 84, 107, 108, *108*
Great Barrier Reef 77
Great Bear Lake 127
Great Britain 99, 153
Great Slave Lake 127
grebe *134*
greenhouse effect 152, 155, 168–169, *168–169*
Greenland 99, 124
Greenwich Meridian 20, *21*, **182, 183**
Gurla Mandhata, Mt. 71
Gulf Stream 102
gyre 100, *100–101*, 102

H

habitat 114, 122, 154, *154, 155*, 160–161, 174, 178–179, **182**
hail 44, *45*, 46, *46*, 48, *124*
Hawaii 113
Hawaiian Islands 76
heat energy 105, 168, *168*

helium 6, 8, 10, 26
herbivore 132, **182**
high pressure *30*, 31, 32, *34*, 34–35, 36, 53, 55, **180**
Himalayas 74, 161, **181**
Honshu 99
horse *88*
household waste 172
hoverfly *133*
Huang He River 126
hummingbird 132, 139
hunger 140, 144, 147
Huron, Lake 127
hurricane 50–51, 55
hydroelectric power 150, 161
hydrogen 6, 8, 10, 26

I

ice cap 124, 125
ice crystals 44–45, *45*, **180**
igneous rock 62–63, 68, **182, 184**
ignimbrite *64*
import 148
incinerator 170–171, 172
India 53, 73, 146, 153
Indian Ocean 53, *53*, 92, 102
Indo-Australian plate 74
Indus River 126
industrial waste 170–171
industrialization 148, 149, 164, 168, 170
industrialized country **182**
insect *154, 155*
International Date Line 20, *21*
intrusive rocks 62–63, *64*
ionosphere *26*, 28
iron 6, 58, *59*, 83, 129, **180**
island 76–77, 174
isobar 55, **183**
ivory poacher 175, 178

J

Jupiter 8, *8, 9*

K

kagu *176*
Kalahari Desert 44, 118
Kamet, Mt. 71
Kanchenjunga, Mt. 71
Kenya wildlife conservation 178–179
khamsin wind 33
King George VI Falls 127
Kungur, Mt. 71
Kuroshio 102

L

Labrador Current *101*
laccolith *63*
lakes 127, 167
landscape 61, 67
latitude 116, **183**
Laurasia 73, *73*
lava *62*, 63, **184**
lead 83
leaf 130, *131*, *133*, *163*
Lena River 126
leopard *132*, 175
Le Puy volcano *62*
leucaena tree 162, *163*
leukemia 156
life 6, 8, 10, 129
lightning 47, *47*, 48, *48*
light-year 11, **183**
limestone 65–66, 67, *67*, *68*, 69, 77, 89
lithosphere 58, **183**
London 145, **182**
longitude 20, **182, 183**
longshore drift *105*
Los Angeles 145, *164*, 166
low pressure *30*, 31, 32, 33, 34–35, *35*, 37, 53, *53*, 54, **181**
Luna spacecraft 14
lunar **183**
lunar eclipse 16, *17*
Lystrosaurus 72

M

Mackenzie River 126
Madagascar 73, *99*
Madeira River 126
magma 62, *62–63*, 63,
74, 77, **183**, **184**
magnesium *59*
magnetic field 84
magnetometer 84
Makalu, Mt. 71
malaria 138, 155, 158
mantle **183**, **184**
manufacturing 149, 150,
170, **182**
Maracaibo, Lake 127
marble *68*, 69, *69*
Mardalsfossen Falls 127
Mare **184**
marine **184**
Mars 8, *8*, *9*
Mediterranean climate
116–117, *119*
Mediterranean Sea 33,
90
Mekong River 126
Mercury 8, *8*, *9*
Mesosaurus 72
metals 83
metamorphic rocks
68–69, *68–69*, **184**
metamorphism 68
meteor *27*, **184**
Meteor Crater 28
meteorologist **184**
meteorology 54–55
methane 24
Mexico 153
Michigan, Lake 127
mid-ocean ridge *74*, 92,
93
Milky Way 10–11, *11*
minerals 83, 148–149
Mississippi River 126
Mississippi–Missouri
River 126
Missouri River 126
mist 40, 41, *54*
Mojave Desert 118
Mombassa 147
Mongefossen Falls 127
monsoon 52–53, *116*,
119, 161

moon 10, 12–15, *15*,
183, **184**, **185**
cycles 108, *108*
eclipse 16, *17*
landing 14–15, *14*
phases *12–13*, 13–14
moorland 67
moraine *70–71*
mountain 41, *41*, 78, *78*,
92
mountain climate *116*,
119
mountain plants *120*,
122
Murray-Darling River
126
mudstone 65, 69

N

Nairobi 147
Namcha Barwa, Mt. 71
Namibia 118, 121
Nanda Devi, Mt. 71
Nanga Parbat, Mt. 71
Nappe and thrust fault
79
nature reserve *179*
Nazca plate *74*, *76*, 94,
94
Neptune 8, *9*
Netherlands 153
New Guinea *99*
nickel 6, 58, **180**
Niger River 126
Nile 126
nimbostratus cloud 38,
39, 43, *43*
nitrogen 26, 129, *163*
nitrogen oxide 164, *166*,
167, **180**
North America 33, *73*,
111, *168*
North American plate *74*
North Atlantic Current
118
North Atlantic gyre *100*,
102
Northern Hemisphere 19,
22, *22*, 28, 31, 33, 34,
102, *116*
northern lights 28
North Indian gyre *101*

North Pacific gyre *100*
North Pole 19, *19*, 22
nuclear power 150, 171
nuclear reaction 6, 10

O

Ob-Irtysh River 126
obsidian *64*
occluded front 37, *37*, *54*
ocean 6, 90, *94*, *124*
basin 74, 92
current 33, 53,
100–101, 102, *105*
exploration 95–96,
95–97
mid-ocean ridges
74–75, *74*, 92, *93*
oceanography 90
Ocean Thermal Energy
Conservation 113
ocean waves 104–105,
105
oil 83, 84, *84–85*, 89,
149, 150, 152
Ontario, Lake 127
ore 83, 84
over-population 146,
147, 157
oxides 164, *166*, 167
oxygen 24, 26, *59*, 129,
130, 155
ozone 24, 165
ozone layer *27*, *55*

P

Pacific Ocean 33, 72, 75,
92, 94, *94*, *103*, **182**
Pacific plate *74*, *76*, *94*
paleontologist **184**
Pangaea 72, 73
Paraná River 126
parasite 137–138, **184**
penumbra *16*
peridotite *59*
Peru 103
Peru-Chile Trench *76*
pesticides 134
photosynthesis 24, *129*,
130, *130*, **180**, **184**
planets 6, 8, *8–9*, 11
orbit *9*

plants   24, 120, *120*, 129, *129*, 130:
  evolution   88, 89
  extinct   177, *177*
  habitat   114, 122, 154, *154*, 155, *155*
  parasite   137
  partnership   138–139
  reserve   *179*
plate tectonics   74–75, 76–77, *76*, *79*, 80
Pluto   8, *9*
polar easterlies   *30*, 31
polar front   36, *36*
polar region   42, 100, 102, 116, *116*, *119*, 169, **180**
polar zone   23, 28, *29*, 31
pollution:
  air   149, 152, *164*, 164–167, *166*
  industrial   170–171
  pesticides   134, *134*
polystyrene   *165*
population   140, 142–147, 157
potassium   *59*
power *see* energy
power station   106, *106*, 109, 113, 149, 168, 171
precipitation   44–45, *124*, **184**
predator   **184**
prospecting   83–85

Q

quartz   63
quinine   155–156

R

radioactive waste   171–172
rafflesia   137, *137*
rain   38, 39, *39*, *44*, 44–45, 47, *54*, *119*, 120, *124*
rainbow   28
rain forest   120, 154–159
rainwater   67, **180**
Rakaposhi, Mt.   71
recycling   128, *129*, 172

Red Sea   72, 78, *94*
refrigerator   *165*
Reichenbach Falls   127
renewable   **184**
reptile   *154*, *155*
rhyolite   *64*
Ribbon Falls   127
Riccioli's Moon map   *15*
Richter scale   81
rift valley   78, *78*, 79, 92, *93*, **184**
Ring of Fire   75
Rio de Janeiro   *146*
rip current   *105*
rivers   126
rock   56, 61–69
  cycle   70, *70*
  dating   89
  folding and faulting   78–79
rock prospecting   83–85
Rocky Mountains   33
Rudolf, Lake   *127*

S

Sahara Desert   29, 44, 118
salt   83, 84, *85*
sand dune   162
sandstone   65, 67, *67*, *79*, 89
satellite   **184**
  weather   55
Saturn   8, *9*
savanna zone   *116*, *119*, *121*
scavenger   **185**
Scottish Highlands   61, 69, 79
sea *see* ocean
sea, inland   127
sea level   169, *169*
seasons   22–23, *22–23*
sedimentary rocks   65, *65*, *67*, 68, **182**, **184**, **185**
seismograph   81, *82*
sewage   172
shadow zone   82, *82*
shale   *68*, 69, 89
shooting star   28, **184**
side-scan sonar   95–96
silicon   *59*

silt   65
Silver Strand Falls   127
sirocco wind   33
slash and burn agriculture   155, 156–157, *157*
slate   *68*, 69
sleet   46
smog   *164*, 165–166
snake   174
snow   38, 44–46, *54*, 116, *124*, *166*, 167
snowflake   45, 46, *46*
Society Islands   76, *76*
sodium   *59*
soil   122, *122–123*, *125*, 156, 159, 160–162, *163*, *166*, 167, 174
solar   **185**
solar eclipse   16, *16*
solar energy   168, *168*
solar heating   30
solar particles   *27*, 28, **180**
solar power   152, 153
Solar System   6, *8–9*, 10, 11
solstice   22
South Africa   33, 148
South America   73, 102, 149
South American plate   *74*
South Atlantic gyre   *100*
Southern Hemisphere   22–23, 28, 31, 33, 34, 102, *103*
South Indian gyre   *100*
South Pacific gyre   *100*
South Pole   *18*, 19, *19*
Southwest Monsoon   53
Soviet Union *see* USSR
Space photography   14
Space probe   14
Spain   153
spring   22, *22*, 23
spring tide   108, *108*
Sri Lanka   174
stalactite   *66*, 67
stalagmite   *66*, 67
standard of living   146–148
stars   10, 11
static electricity   47–48

steppe zone *116, 119, 120*

storms 50–52, *51*

strata **185**

stratocumulus cloud *43*

stratosphere *26*

stratus cloud *39, 43*

subduction zone **185**

subtropical zone *116, 119*

Sudan 162

sulfur 83, *166*, 167

sulfur oxide 164, *166*, **180**

Sumatra 99

summer *18*, 22, *22*, 23, 35

sun 6, 9, 10, *10*, 11, 29:
    eclipse 16, *16*
    rays *29, 168*
    tide 108, *108*

Superior, Lake 127

sustainable **185**

Sutherland Falls 127

T

Table Mountain *41*

Tahiti *76*, 107

Taiga *116, 119*

Tanganyika, Lake 127

Tasmanian wolf 177

temperate zones 23, *29*, 31, 44, 116, *116*, 118, *119*, 120, *120*, 122

temperature 29, *29*, 54, 168, *168*, *169*

temperature patterns *119*

terrace farming 161

Thailand 149

Third World *see* developing countries

thunder *39*, 48–49, **181**

tidal power 109

tidal wave **185**

tide 13, 107–108, *108*

tiger 175

time 18–19, *18–19*

time zones 20–21, **182**

Tirich Mir, Mt. 71

Titanic 101

Tonga Trench *76*

tornado 51–52

trade wind *30*, 31, 32, 118

transpiration *124*, **185**

trawl net 111, *111*, **185**

tree *120*, 137, 138, 151, 162, *163*
    see also forest; forest destruction

trench, ocean 74, *76*

tropical forest 120, 154–159, *155, 163*, 177

tropical zone 23, *29*, 30, 42, 44, 45, 51, *116, 117, 119, 120*, 122

Tropic of Cancer *18, 19*

Tropic of Capricorn *19*

troposphere *26*, 42

tsunamis *81*, **185**

Tugela Falls 127

tundra 23, *120, 122*

turbine 106, *106*, 109

typhoon 51

Tyssefallene Falls 127

U

Ulugh Muztagh, Mt. 71

umbra *16*

underwater exploration *95*, 95–96, *96–97*

United Nations Food and Agricultural Organization 110, 151, 159

United States 148, 149

uranium 171

Uranus 8, *9*

urbanization 147, *147*, **185**

USSR 148, 149

V

vapor 26, 29, 40–41, 168

vegetation zones 120, *120*

Venus 8, *8*, 9

Victoria, Lake 127

Victoria Island 99

volcano *62*, 63, 75, *75*, **182, 185**

volcanic island 77, *77*

Volga River 126

vulture 132

W

waning **185**

warm front 37, *37*, 38, *39, 54*, 55

water contamination *134*, 170–172

water cycle 124–125

waterfalls 127

water pollution *166*, 167, 170–172

water power 105–106, 152

waves 104–105, *105*

weather 26, *26*, 29–33, 116, *116*
    depression 37
    fronts 38–39, *39*
    high and low pressure 34–35
    records 32, 44
    systems 36, *39*, 50, 54, **180, 181**

weather code *54*, 55

weather forecasting 54–55, *54*

westerlies *30*, 31, 32, 118

wildebeest 14

wildlife 174–177

wildlife conservation 178, 179

wind 30–33, *30, 32–33, 54*, 116

wind power 152–153

wind storm 50–53

Winnipeg, Lake 127

winter 22, *22*, 23, 35

wood 151, 152, 153, *163*

Y

Yangtze River 126

Yenisey River 126

Yosemite Falls 127

Z

Zaire River 126

ACKNOWLEDGMENTS

The publishers wish to thank the following for supplying photographs for this book:

Page 3 ZEFA; 7 NASA; 11 Science Photo Library; 14 NASA; 15 Ann Ronan Picture Library; 16 ZEFA; 19 NHPA/S. Krasemann; 23 NHPA/S. Krasemann (right), Biofotos (left); 25 ZEFA; 28 ZEFA; 31 Dennis Gilbert; 39 University of Dundee, Crown Copyright; 41 Camera Press; 46 NHPA/J. Shaw; 47 ZEFA; 49 Frank Lane Picture Agency; 51 NOAA; 52 A.G.E Fotostock; 55 Science Photo Library; 57 ZEFA; 59 Imitor; 60 Salt Lake Convention; 61 ZEFA; 62 ZEFA; 64 Imitor; 65 NHPA/G. I. Bernard; 67 ZEFA (top), Imitor (bottom); 68 Imitor; 69 ZEFA (top), Imitor (bottom); 77 ZEFA; 79 Nature Photographers; 81 A.G.E. Fotostock; 83 Shell; 85 Shell; 86 Imitor; 87 Imitor; 91 A.G.E. Fotostock; 94 Science Photo Library; 95 Institute of Oceanographic Services; 97 Science Photo Library; 98 ZEFA; 104 Dennis Gilbert; 107 ZEFA; 109 Valan Photos; 110 ZEFA; 112 Shell; 115 ZEFA; 117 ZEFA; 118 NHPA/J. Shaw; 121 NHPA/A. Bannister; 126 NHPA/E. A. Janes; 128 Nature Photographers; 132 NHPA/P. Johnson; 135 ZEFA; 136 Bruce Coleman Ltd; 141 ZEFA; 144 ZEFA; 145 Panos Pictures; 146 ZEFA; 148 ZEFA; 149 ZEFA; 150 The Hutchison Library; 152 Science Photo Library; 153 Science Photo Library; 154 NHPA/E. A. MacAndrew; 157 Bruce Coleman Ltd; 158 South American Pictures; 160 Bruce Coleman Ltd; 162 FAO; 164 ZEFA; 167 NHPA/J. Shaw; 170 Friends of the Earth; 171 Nature Photographers; 172 Greenpeace; 173 Frank Lane Picture Agency; 174 NHPA/M. Wendler; 175 Nature Photographers; 176 NHPA/M. Wendler (top), Frank Lane Picture Agency (bottom); 178 Camera Press; 181 FAO; Cover ZEFA, Spectrum, NHPA.

Illustrations by Hardlines (pp.119, 169); Hayward Artists (pp. 70–71, 78–79, 84–85, 87, 96, 124–125, 166–167, 168); Gillian Kenny (Linden Artists, p. 163); Janos Marphy (Middleton Artists, pp. 8–9, 10, 11, 12–13, 16, 17, 34, 35, 38–39, 44–45, 48–49, 50, 76, 92–93; Ian Moores (pp. 159, 165, 173); Jane Pickering (Linden Artists, p. 156); Sebastian Quigley (Linden Artists, pp. 74–75, 76); Mike Saunders (Middleton Artists, pp. 97, 106, 111, 112, 113, 122–123, 129, 134, 137, 161); Nick Shewring (The Garden Studio, pp. 18, 19, 20–21, 22, 29, 30, 32, 36, 37, 40, 51, 53, 54, 72, 73, 80, 81, 82, 94, 99, 101, 103, 105, 126, 127, 130, 135, 155, 179); Brian Watson (Linden Artists, pp. 32–33, 100–101, 102–103, 116–117, 120–121, 142–143, 150–151, 169).